FIREGAL...

RISING FROM THE ASHES

BY GINA L. GELDBACH-HALL

[handwritten inscription:] MEAD Session

Noel yourself
Empower your
& ignite your
own flame.
Enjoy !!!
Gina L. Geldbach-Hall

About the Cover

Sometimes you just know when something is right. It starts in your gut–a knowingness that makes sense, if only to you. That was this cover. I actually had the cover designed about the time I was finishing my first draft. I contacted my graphic artist, showed her this picture of me in my turn-out pants, and asked her to design a cover with this picture on it. I took this photo in 2007, as part of a boudoir photo shoot, totally unrelated to this book. I didn't realize it at the time, but those photos liberated me in a way that I had not been liberated before.

That photo on the cover became a part of one of the six panels of pictures I still have hanging in my bedroom. I look at these photos and I remind myself that I am a woman–sexy, vivacious, and alive. Some have criticized the photo as being too risqué for a book that talks about discrimination and women's rights. I disagree. I think the value we bring as women to any part of this world is valued and valuable. This cover has come to mean being totally me, in a very male-dominated profession, while still maintaining a sense of my feminine essence. As I worked from coming out of the darkness (the black background symbolized on the cover) to the light (the white part of the cover), I had to peel away those layers of myself I had hidden and really embrace the woman I am today. This book symbolizes that journey, sometimes ugly, sometimes traumatic, but always changing, helping me see the beauty that was always a part of me. Whether I was being a firefighter, a mother, or a woman, I had to come to a place where I honored me in whatever I was doing. Today, I still struggle with finding my place in this world in a vulnerable, feminine way. It's a journey that may take a lifetime but that's okay. I know I'll make it.

So, I thank the women that make my cover a success and provide yet another testament to the beauty of women everywhere. Thank you, Victoria Hart, of Pink Kitty Designs, for your beautiful book cover design; Jennifer Johnson of J and J Photography for capturing the vulnerable, yet very core essence of me on the cover; Sue Altenburg of Altenburg Studios, (back cover photo) for giving the world another view of me through the eye of the camera; and Amelia Cooper-Cline of Amelia C & Co (Hair and Makeup Artistry- back photo) and Nina Ament (makeup artistry- front photo) for making me absolutely glow. I envy all of your skills in making people look beautiful and radiant. I know I am forever changed by your eye and your camera lens . . .

Dedication

This book is lovingly dedicated to my friend, fellow firefighter, and classmate, Lari McSwain. She was a powerhouse of a woman and a trailblazer, afraid of nothing, or so she made it seem! As I wrote these pages, I was reminded of how much I miss her and how Lari inspired everyone she touched including me. She encouraged and taught me to reach for more, be happy, and the true value of having a life bigger than work.

Lari, you are so missed by everyone who knew you. Your light shone brightly on all of us and I am honored to have basked in it while you were here. . .

Lari McSwain
December 2, 1963 to April 19, 2010

About the Cover   *v*

Dedication   *vii*

Prelude   *xi*

Prologue   *xv*

Section 1   **How it all began . . .**   **1**

Chapter 1   *The first step . . .*   *3*

Chapter 2   *Rookie school education*   *13*

Chapter 3   *It doesn't always take a super hero . . .* *19*

Chapter 4   *My story*   *25*

Section 2   **Emotional rollercoaster**   **51**

Chapter 5   *Choosing the right path . . .*   *53*

Chapter 6   *Into the looking glass*   *59*

Chapter 7   *Size-up*   *69*

Chapter 8   *When life hands you a toilet brush . . .* *81*

Chapter 9   *Are those tears?*   *103*

Chapter 10   *Change happens . . .*   *129*

Chapter 11   *Put down the remote!*   *139*

Chapter 12   *Wear it proudly . . .*   *151*

Chapter 13   *WORK is a 4-letter word*   *161*

Chapter 14   *Getting out of my own way!*   *167*

Chapter 15	*Walking the talk*	*175*

Section 3	**What to do when it's over**	**185**

Chapter 16	*The choir of heavenly angels*	*187*

Section 4	**Do you really have what it takes?**	**195**

Chapter 17	*Really seeing the dog*	*197*
Chapter 18	*But would I do it again?*	*205*
Chapter 19	*Riding it out to hope . . .*	*213*
Chapter 20	*What if you don't win?*	*223*

Section 5	**Have a life outside your department**	**229**

Chapter 21	*The job is not your life!*	*231*

Epilogue		*237*
Acknowledgments		*239*
About the Author		*243*

***While being a** firefighter is such a thrilling and rewarding life, you need to keep in mind that you are but one piece of a giant puzzle that when put together properly makes an amazing picture.*

~*Allen B. Locklier, Jr*
author of "On Call"

As we raced along a blacktop road to a horrific explosion, it hardly seemed like we had just been lounging around the firehouse only moments before. Actually, the day had been like most days at our fire station—a few medical calls and responses—some maintenance tasks to keep us busy, just another ordinary shift. We finished testing hydrants between calls and headed back to the station for lunch, anticipating more of the same that afternoon. After lunch, we all went off to our corners to take a nap, watch some TV, do whatever someone does during their hour of down time. Taking a few precious minutes to relax, I had almost dozed off, when we all heard a loud crash. Thinking someone had run their vehicle into our barn door (where we park the fire trucks), we all jumped up in surprise and bolted towards the barn to see what was going on.

Finding everything intact, bewildered and scratching our heads, we all returned to the day room. Just as we began to settle back in, it happened again—except this time, it sounded more like a sonic boom. You could hear the rattle and see the plate glass window that covered the entire front entry shake. In that surreal second, no one spoke. The anticipation of what was about to come was palpable. Once again, we started toward the barn, this time to gear up and put on our turnouts (our protective coveralls). We all knew without saying a word that whatever produced such an explosion was going to be profound and we were going to be working. Just as I finished putting on my turnouts, the alarm tones started. This would be a multiple-alarm fire.

Pepcon had just exploded.

It was 1988, and I was assigned to Station 20. At the time, we had an engine and hose wagon at our station. On most days, we had five personnel on duty: one captain, two engineers (one who drove the hose wagon) and two firefighters. Station 20 was located in the far northeast part of the Las Vegas valley. The Pepcon plant produced rocket fuel for the space shuttle and was located in Henderson, Nevada—at the extreme southeast part of the same valley, some 15 miles away. As the engine pulled out of the barn, a plume of smoke that became our homing beacon was visible in the distance.

We had one of the oldest engines still in use at the time and the only one where firefighters still rode on the tailboard. Yet, back then, the same engine was progressive in that it was one of the few in the department's fleet that had a speaker on the back, which allowed firefighters to monitor dispatch traffic and hear, in real-time, the magnitude of the emergency response to the explosion. We took Boulder Highway out to the Pepcon plant site. As we drove, the chatter and commands coming from dispatch were never-ending and we were hearing that there could be hundreds of casualties, including the dead and missing, with more explosions possible.

At that point, I had only been on the fire department for 16 months—long enough to have squelched some *good* fires like a few apartment buildings that went up in smoke—but nothing like this. As we approached the scene, I could see the column of smoke and I wondered if I was ready— *really* ready for this. No one was sure what had happened or could still happen. Another blast hit as we were driving Code 3 (with lights and siren) to the disaster. It was becoming all too real.

Boulder Highway, which headed north/south, was a ghost road as you headed south. On this day, however, northbound traffic was packed with hundreds of cars in line leaving Henderson, trying to get as far away from the disaster as they could. White-knuckle fear was etched on the drivers' faces like stadium fans after a report of shots fired, but no one honked or crossed over to take advantage of the opposing lane. The civilized nature of the evacuation just added to the mass anxiety lurking below the surface.

We drove by a casino that was under construction—its windows now blown out from the blasts. It was worse as we got closer to the site—huge signs were blown to the ground; metal sheds were lying on their sides and everything—absolutely everything, was covered in a gray dust. It looked like fallout after a nuclear blast.

I gripped the handrail tighter as thoughts raced through my head. What am I doing here? What did I get myself into? Why am I driving toward a disaster when any reasonable person would be running away? My fellow firefighter and I exchanged a nervous glance and I could see in his eyes the same fear of the unknown. We had no idea what this day had in store for us, but whatever it was, it was going to be a story we would retell for years to come. This was going to be a day we would never forget.

It was the day I became a true firefighter.

PROLOGUE

Adults are always asking children what they want to be when they grow up because they're looking for ideas.

~Paula Poundstone
author & comedian

I'm not always sure why I became a firefighter. My parents have a picture of me at around age 3 in a red fire chief's pushcart. Frankly, I wanted to be a cowgirl for most of my younger years. In retrospect, firefighting was a better choice! I do know I was brought up with two basic ideals drilled into my head. My dad would say to me, "Gina, you can be anything you want to be!" My mom would say, "Gina, never be in a position where you can't take care of yourself or have to rely on a man!" So, who would have thought I would come out stubborn and feeling equal to any man? It never dawned on me February 2nd, 1987, that I wasn't entitled to be starting rookie school. I was being *anything I wanted to be.*

Part of my confidence came from my earlier years growing up as a military dependent. My dad was a career officer in the Air Force. He joined just before I was born, and, retired the year I graduated from high school. I never stayed any place long; the average was about three years. The plus was I saw a lot of the country. The downside was the lack of a home base. As I've aged, I have come to see what a hole that has put in me—the lack of a hometown. It leaves me feeling ungrounded and as my parents age, I feel a sense of loss about where I will go "home" to after they leave this life. I always say my hometown is where my parents live, but I really won't have one after they pass. That's sad. Even though I have lived in Las Vegas for over 30-years and have a wonderful base of friends and family, I long for a root in a place where I can simply walk the dirt and know I was from *there*. Since 9-11, you can't even get onto military bases without a military ID, so even if I wanted to take my children or grandchildren on a tour of my past, I couldn't even enter the gate. My past really dies with my parents . . . Now I alone must define who I am and where I fit into this world. The upside to being a military brat, however, was I got to see the world in a way only afforded to children of the American military.

Growing up as a military dependent had certain advantages. I saw many new places and lived in Europe where my world was flooded with new sights, sounds, and people as the turnstile of military orders kept us on the move. I met some very interesting people and I thought that was "normal." The beauty of life as a military dependent was that I lived a colorblind life. The crowning glory was I truly didn't understand the concept of racism. Most of my friends were of mixed races and I didn't see that as unusual or even a topic of conversation. I really don't remember being exposed to any form of racism until I entered my first public high school when I started 10th grade. I remember my surprise and shock at what people did to be mean for no apparent reason other than a different color of skin or ethnic background. It should be no surprise that my closest friends made in that high school were also military dependents and we didn't even have to look—we just found each other. I think it was as much for our own survival as the fact we had a different perspective on people and life.

My mom was a schoolteacher and so was my dad. He worked part time in the evening teaching math to airmen and others going to school. My mom taught English, so I had the perfect trifecta as a student. Mom helped with all my papers, my dad got me proficient with math, and I was living history through the places we lived. Yep, school was pretty easy for me, and for the most part, enjoyable. Education was a big part of my growing up and a lot of emphasis was placed on doing well at my "job" . . . school. In grade school, I was a really good student and my grades reflected that. In college . . . well, I got my degree! I went to the school of fun and frolic. I also worked full-time through most of it. I got through, but I wouldn't brag about my GPA. My dad imparted a piece of wisdom as I mulled over my grade-point plight one night, he said, "Gina, look at all my diplomas. Do you see my GPA on any of them? Just graduate!" After that talk, my fear of failure passed and with the pressure off, my love of learning returned. In the end, it probably wouldn't have been the walk of shame if my GPA had appeared, but I felt pretty proud of my accomplishment. I still have an insatiable hunger that only continuous study can sate, even if it has been decades since I last earned that degree.

We are usually well on our way to adulthood before we realize the gifts our parents gave us. It wasn't until now that I can truly look back on my upbringing and realize the values of empowerment and capability that were seeded in me as far back as my memories go. Now, older and wiser, I look back and really appreciate that training. I know at the time I started in fire and emergency services, I was naive and I wonder at my willingness to step into the unknown with such a child-like innocence. It never really dawned on me, at the time, women weren't *supposed* to be firefighters. I was offered a job that would make it so I wasn't dependent on a man, I could help people, and loved what I did. I didn't start out seeing how my decision to follow in this path was ripe with both negative and positive consequences; I simply followed my heart.

I am often asked why I chose to go into firefighting. The more appropriate question is, "Why did I *not* think about it?" I mean, why didn't it even occur to me I might not be successful there? I just saw something that I liked and thought would be fun and jumped into it. I didn't know any better and it never really occurred to me I wouldn't succeed. I knew from my life experience that if I really wanted something, I could have it. My dad told me I could, so I did. Anyway, no person could make me quit until *I* decided to!

This book is a snap shot . . . a portrayal of my journey into what makes me tick. It is also a realization of who and what I am and why I didn't quit when at times it would have been so easy and such a release. I had to matter to me; I had to look in that mirror and grab a thread of sanity to pull myself through. It's a combination of my past and present, sometimes in direct conflict with each other, which I had to sort through and find a new perspective and higher vantage point to make sense of what was before me. It was that climb . . . fall . . . and then climb again which really started to define the girl emerging to a woman. This book is as much about overcoming life's twists and turns as it is about a young firefighter and her struggles to make sense of an unjust system. This story is so much more than just surviving discrimination. It's my journey through life's sometimes traumatic events and how I adapted and overcame, emerging a fuller, more complete me on the other side. While this book is my way of making sense, it is not meant as a historical, time lined adventure. No, it's more accurate than that. See, I have found that lessons are rarely cyclic but more circular, coming together when we are ready. In fact, as I wrote, I realized that events spread several years, to even decades apart, coalesced as they come into focus and their meanings understood and integrated. Sometimes my past ended up a greater teacher than I was listener . . . However, when I got, "It," I got it! My story unfolds as a guidebook to my greatest lessons learned and where those lessons originated versus a historical account of my career.

Much of what I say in these pages is not from the pulpit of amenity, rather, a manifest of the things I still work on for myself. I find when I am coaching others I should actually be putting a mirror in front of my face because I need the same advice. As I go deeper into that rabbit hole of the unknown, the lessons become more profound, felt more deeply, and, thankfully, linger for less time. I "get it" faster now and I have become my own guidance counselor. It feels, at times, as if I have two of me; they communicate and debate one another in my head and frequently, it is overwhelming. This 'mind fuck' of mine (my term coined because of its incessant nature, which can feel like torture at times) is the by-product of all my personal work and for that I am grateful. Even though I get frustrated with the process, I appreciate the hard-earned wisdom those discussions provide even if the only attendees are self-created.

Those talks in my head have become old trusted friends, forged from the grit of life's rough and tumbled road. Although it can be very scary to venture out of my comfort zone, I have come to rely on my inner wisdom and intuition to guide me faithfully through whatever comes to dance at my door. I never think of leaving those voices behind, as they come from hard earned, well-healed, and loving advice; I earned every ounce of wisdom they lovingly impart, even if they are frustrating to hear at times.

Life's complicated. It never seems to be a smooth, straight road with no speed bumps or potholes. But honestly, I'm happy for that. It never fails that when I come out of those ruts in the road of life, my life seems eerily happier and less complicated. I guess it's after visiting the ruts and potholes, I now have a road hazard sign marking unsafe conditions which lie ahead so I can safely exit to a detour. More simply, I learned what I wanted, what I didn't want, and I now have a more complete road map to follow. Either way, the pits in life are where the ride gets crazy and I learn to drive a whole lot better . . .

SECTION 1

How it all began . . .

When life throws you a curve and you swing and miss, you have to remember you are still at bat!

~Gina Geldbach-Hall,
author

Faith is taking the first step even when you don't see the whole staircase.

~Martin Luther King Jr.
clergyman & activist

If you had met me in earlier days, you would never have believed I could have become a firefighter. Whenever we responded to the scene of a fire or accident I could see it on people's faces . . . *How can that little thing who looks so girlie be a firefighter?* The reaction was always the same, but how could I blame them? Sometimes I wondered myself.

In 2009, after a career which spanned over 25-years in fire and emergency service, I retired as a battalion chief. As battalion chief, I had supervised 65 out of the 775 employees in the department and had been in charge of 10 fire stations. While I was in this position of authority, I was responsible for making choices and decisions on a regular basis, which could impact other people's lives, the organization, and the community-at-large. Such accountability made me take a good, hard look at myself and in the process; I began to ask myself, "What will my legacy be? What will I leave behind that will make this world a better and safer place for my children?" Recently, my son, Joe, told me that he wants to become a firefighter. That really means something to me and to his father, who is also a firefighter. Joe's announcement made me think back to my beginnings in the fire service and how I came to the decision of becoming one myself.

My becoming a firefighter was more of a fluke than a decision. I was in college and looking for a job when I happened upon a newspaper ad for a private transport company looking for someone to handle their advertising. I applied, was hired, and immediately began to learn about politics. Politics, at its core, is about the sharing of information and the motivations behind it. As I began to learn my job, it seemed the company didn't so much need advertising to increase their business, as they needed a decent bookkeeper to handle their accounts payable and receivable. At the time, I was too young and naive to realize they never intended the company to turn a profit. I didn't understand about shielding income from the IRS. Therefore, when I took the company from a 60% collection rate to a 99% collection rate in just three months, as you might imagine, they were less than pleased. I, of course, was clueless as to why the boss didn't seem to appreciate my efforts or even like me. That realization didn't occur until years later, after I learned about profit sharing, revenue reporting, and taxation.

The company specialized in nonemergency medical transports. One of the selling or *advertising* points for this company was that they would have an EMT (Emergency Medical Technician) on each vehicle to render aid in case a client (i.e. patient) needed care during transport. It seemed they were always short on drivers, which created challenges in scheduling. About five months after I was hired, our sister-company, an ambulance service, offered an EMT class and my managers invited me to attend free. After just one week of classes, I knew I was going to love responding to emergencies and helping people get the services they needed.

I sat in class, absorbing information like a sponge. I literally soaked up the training on how to respond to emergency calls, perform certain medical procedures, and transport patients to the hospital in accordance with the established protocols and guidelines. I was learning everything from the life-saving technique of maintaining an open airway to ensure adequate breathing and cardiopulmonary resuscitation (CPR), to how to control external bleeding, prevent shock, splint a bone fracture, and immobilize a patient to prevent spinal damage. All of this was exciting and powerful for me. I felt like I was going to get the opportunity to do something really important and I couldn't get enough. With each lesson and assignment, I felt more alive, and I couldn't wait to put all that new knowledge to practical use.

After finishing the EMT course, the company allowed me to work as a backup driver, which eventually led to more driving than office work. That was okay, because with the company showing a profit, they wanted to get me as far away from the accounting department as possible. Shortly thereafter, I made a permanent switch from the non-emergency side of transportation to ambulances. The variety and fast pace of life as an emergency responder impassioned me.

My very first call was a vehicular trauma where I needed to perform life-saving measures. My second call was a cardiac arrest. I soon learned that such activity was considered a *good* day in the ambulance business. Though I didn't get to find out if either person survived, I do know that without our care they would not have even had a chance. I began to get more experience with each shift. It was exciting, stimulating, scary, and frustrating—an adrenaline-pumping, rock-n-roll type of sensation that renewed itself every 24-hours. Plus, I was making more money than I had ever made, meeting more interesting people than I had ever met, and partying more than I could ever have imagined. It was sensational.

Could there have possibly been a better job in the world? I loved being on the front lines and I began to see a future for myself. Rapidly, my career was being crystalized with clarity and allure and being a girlie-girl was not an option, as I often had to lift some heavy patients onto gurneys. I started to lift weights to increase my strength during my time off to make sure I could carry my own weight, so to speak. However, none of this seemed to line up with my current educational path. At that point, after attending years of classes, I was about to get my bachelor's degree in Business and Advertising, which put me at a crossroads. Should I listen to my head and move into a field like marketing and advertising that was sustainable over time, or should I follow my heart and pursue a career in emergency services? I was just considering attending a program that taught para-medicine in Oregon, when I heard that the local fire department was testing for new recruits.

Brent, my boyfriend at the time (who later became my husband), suggested that we take the test together and I figured, "What the heck?" I wasn't really interested in advertising anyway and I could make more money as a beginning firefighter than I would after five years of climbing the corporate ladder. I also wasn't thrilled about leaving my boyfriend to attend months of training in another state. I remember thinking, "How hard could this written test be anyway?" After all, I was just finishing up college. As for the physical portion of the test, I wasn't so sure even though I was transporting medical emergencies on a regular basis which required that I dead-lift patients into the back of the ambulance. I had a 300-pound patient limit before I needed to ask for assistance from more than my partner. Back then, they didn't have all the fancy lift-assist to load patients into the back of the ambulance that they have today. After lifting ten or more patients a day, plus working out at the gym, I figured the physical agility test for the fire department was do-able but I still had doubts. I had heard all too many times, from both men and women alike, about their dashed hopes in not passing the fire department's performance exam and the pain that went with it.

There were several phases of the fire department's testing for new recruit candidates. The most difficult hurdle I faced ended up being an exercise where I had to join together two couplings (which are the male/female threaded counterparts that connect one fire hose to another) within a two minute and thirty second time frame. It was a single elimination test—there were no do-overs. At the time, I was not familiar with the fire deluge system, which is a piece of equipment that intakes a larger hose and splits into multiple working lines. I didn't know the male part of one coupling, threaded with a higbee cut, required that I first rotate its outside thread back one-quarter turn before threading it to the female coupling to avoid crossing or mutilation of the threads. This quarter back-turn makes the coupling threads slide right into place. Unfortunately, at the time, I had no idea what I was doing, so I struggled, trying various combinations to adjoin the conflicting factions together. The exercise required a hand-eye coordination, which I did not yet possess, and I felt like I was wearing a pair of clown gloves. I could feel the sweat begin to pour down my face as I saw my future quickly slipping away. Then, by some miracle, it happened- I got it! The two couplings joined in holy matrimony. One by one, I coupled all four of the pairs on the deluge device completing the exercise in *exactly* two minutes and thirty seconds.

Some of the other practical exercises included moving stacks of 2 ½-inch rolled hose, raising ladders, pulling out a 100 foot crosslay, and climbing to the top of a 75 foot aerial ladder where I had to clip in and then lean back, spreading my arms, placing all my trust in the integrity of the unfamiliar safety gear. I completed those exercises with time to spare. At the conclusion of the testing, the fire department scored all the candidates and placed us on an eligibility list. There were 5,000 people who tested for the fire department during that recruitment in October 1986. I didn't know how many people were above me on the list; I just knew that I had passed the same tests, with the same physical requirements, and within the same time limits that the men had. All that remained between getting the job was a chief's interview, which would inevitably come when they reached my name on the list.

Then I waited. Months passed. Then, out-of-the-blue one day in January 1987, I got a call from our dispatcher at the ambulance company that I needed to report to the office right away (back then cell phones were uncommon). They told me the fire department had called for an interview. I couldn't believe it! I called the Fire Chief's secretary, half-believing I was being set up for a practical joke—which was common among the ambulance staff. She was the kindest person you would ever want to know and convinced me that of the 25 people selected, I was one of them! My interview was scheduled for the following week.

I bought a new black suit with matching high-heeled pumps and showed up looking professional. I was excited and anxious at the same time about the prospect of becoming a firefighter. The secretary escorted me into the Fire Chief's office, and I took a seat across from a man who seemed to command respect by his mere presence. He reminded me of someone you might see in a cigar ad, burly and gruff, who could use the heads of small children to extinguish his smoldering embers. He was intimidating at best. My chair sunk in as I sat down. I suddenly felt like a little girl sitting at the grown-up's table.

The Chief asked me questions about my qualifications to be a firefighter. I spoke of the emergency calls I had gone on and the people who I had assisted and saved. Despite my best answers, I was met with a simmering low-level look of disapproval. I began feeling more inadequate as the interview progressed. It seemed nothing I said was well received. The Chief looked at me as if I had killed his dog or something. He clearly did not like me. In the course of the interview, I began to wonder if I really wanted to work for someone like this. It seemed the interview was a disaster of biblical proportions. At the end of a silence which seemed to drag on for an undeterminable amount of time, he dismissed me with a, "That will be all." I slunk out of his office assuming my dreams dashed.

I replayed that interview over in my head a dozen times—even years later—and still can't figure out why it seemed to have gone so awry. In retrospect, back in 1987, females were still a novelty in the fire service nationwide and their numbers easily counted. I suspect the Fire Chief had already considered the impact of hiring more females and the disruption it represented to his fire world—a long-standing, male-dominated culture. As he looked across his huge desk at me, he couldn't help but think of the changes that I, and other women, represented.

You can imagine my surprise when I got a call the following week advising me that I had been selected. Rookie school started on February 2, 1987, and thus, my official life as a firefighter began.

To the uneducated, an A is just three sticks.

~A.A. Milne
English author

Sometimes you look back on your life and realize how unprepared you were for a particular challenge. I don't know if it was due to overconfidence or naiveté, but my first day of rookie school was nothing short of ridiculous. I showed up wearing my favorite white jumpsuit because I wanted to look, well . . . nice for my first day on the job. Discretely, they pulled me aside and advised me I was slightly overdressed. Oh sure, my instructors were nice to me, offering to allow me to opt out of the physical exercises that first day, but I knew enough to realize that such a move would have put a big red target on my back from the very start. No, that day I did everything my male counterparts did and I have the stains to prove it. As for the white jumpsuit? Well, it was a casualty of rookie school and a lesson learned. Note to self, *next time, ask someone.*

Rookie school is basically firefighter boot camp and back then, it lasted for ten weeks. Currently, it spans five months, which is double the training time we had in 1987. Out of a total of 5000 applicants, 40 of which were women, there were only six women who had passed the performance-based tests, interview, and background investigation. Four of the six women were in my class of 25 recruits. Up to that point, the fire department had hired only one other female firefighter (five years earlier), so we were definitely the minority. When we walked into the training room that first day, they had no clue how to handle us. To them, we were a foreign species that had landed on their planet.

The four of us women bonded immediately because nothing can bind souls quicker than a shared sense of misery. The first gender hurdle we had to face came during the first days of training–hair. Luckily, I had short hair, so getting it up off the collar was not an issue for me. The other three women enjoyed long hair down to the middle of their backs, and they were *very* adamant about not cutting it. A quick compromise with the department was reached, and the other women agreed to keep their hair pinned up at all times during their academy training.

Then, there were the bathrooms. The men had a locker room with a shower facility and multiple toilets. The women, on the other hand, enjoyed no such luxury. The four of us became extremely close, both in familiarity and in proximity, as we shared one toilet and a sink in a room no bigger than a broom closet. To make matters even more complicated, we had to share it with the secretarial staff. Like contortionists in a hurry to get out, we struggled to change and get to the blacktop for physical training drills within the time frame allowed. It was not pretty, and the administration frequently forgot about the space limitations and cited us for being tardy.

Physical training was just part of what we needed to do to prepare to fight fires. Hours of classroom time is spent learning about basic construction and operation of doors, windows and locks, which would allow us force entry into a structure or vehicle. We learned about chemical safety and storage, personal protective equipment, safety measures, Occupational Safety and Health Administration (OSHA) laws and regulations, and how oxygen concentration relates to life safety and fire growth. Having just graduated from college, I felt confident in my ability to learn, retain, and be tested on all of the new material we were expected to absorb. I was as focused on learning how to fight fires as I had been in learning emergency response and rescue.

The cadre staff told us on the very first day of class that our seniority at graduation (which later affects your ability to get choice assignments) would be based solely on our mid-term and final examination grades. I was pretty confident I could score in the top percentile, but I still took detailed notes and studied long hours to reinforce my learning and retention about fire suppression, prevention, ventilation, communications, safety, and use of equipment. I spent hours reinforcing lessons taught on structural integrity and how different variables can affect fire behaviors, such as backdrafts and flashovers, which could result in explosions and other dangerous situations. Lastly, I learned about the psychological effects of fighting fires in obscured conditions, as well as the importance of teamwork. All of that effort was starting to pay off as it started to sink in.

Then came the mid-term.

Another woman and I came out as the top two in the class! I was on top of the world and halfway to the "promised land." Then suddenly, the rules changed, and the cadre announced that instead of basing the class members' seniority solely on test scores, they would instead base it on an average of *all* of our scores, which included the more subjective performance-based examinations. In the new scenario, some of our grades were now based on the instructor's *impressions* of a recruit's performance. Clearly, the men had the perceptual upper hand in upper body strength and physical size along with perceived familiarity with the skills required to be successful (e.g., familiarity with hand tools, tying knots and climbing ladders). I became painfully aware that the women had to meet the same performance standards as the men, but should *not* outshine them. This was not the last time the standards or criteria was changed to suit the department's wishes.

In some ways, rookie school was the best of times, but it was also the worst of times. Physically, it pushed me beyond any limits I knew existed. I was proud of my accomplishments and performance and I felt fortunate in making some friends that would last a lifetime. There was something about being together in the presence of fear and danger and working as a team to accomplish something significant—like saving lives or property—that bonds you. However, it can also tear you down.

I'm sorry to say that in those early days, several of my male colleagues had a different idea of where we women belonged in fire fighting. Entering a room at the fire station sometimes left me feeling like the ex-girlfriend who showed up uninvited at the wedding. To be successful in rookie school, it seemed that the men simply needed to avoid stepping on their own two feet, whereas we women had to constantly prove ourselves and our physical capabilities. I had to make a conscious decision to avoid the temptation to walk and talk like the guys in order to maintain some sense of femininity in such a male-dominated culture outside of work. It was hard to turn it on and off. The pressure to conform was extreme and I desperately wanted to fit in, if even only to avoid being singled out.

I never understood the term "harassment" until I joined the fire service. Oh sure, I enjoyed a good joke or a little teasing as much as the next person, but this was like nothing I had ever experienced before. Years later, my attorney told me that harassment is like death by a thousand cuts. I understood that as their comments, innuendos, and treatment over time left me feeling that I was bleeding out from those constant pinpricks.

Being a trail-blazing pioneer is not always what it's cracked up to be nor is it something I thought I would have to face by simply making the decision to join the fire department. It can get very lonely out on the skinny branches of life taking a stand for yourself, even lonelier if you aren't prepared for the journey you unexpectedly find yourself propelled into. Sometimes, change comes about easily but other times you have to fight for it, yet sometimes the fight simply finds you. If there is one thing I have learned, *it's you can't be successful . . . unless you're uncomfortable.* In that discomfort, I found a part of myself I didn't even know existed and as I write, I endeavor to share the experience so others who follow will have a roadmap, something I would have loved to have had as I went down this path of integration. Thus, here is where the story of transformation begins—the story of how the fire department changed the way they treated their female firefighters and how it forever changed me.

CHAPTER 3

It doesn't always take a super hero...

True heroism is remarkably sober, very undramatic. It is not the urge to surpass all others at whatever cost, but the urge to serve others at whatever cost.

~Arthur Ashe
tennis player

Every kid has a hero. Most of the people heralded as heroes in our society today tend to be athletes, entertainers, or politicians. In actuality, I believe the majority of heroes start out as just plain regular folks. They will never receive a Heisman Trophy, or an Academy Award, or a Pulitzer Prize, and yet their actions leave a footprint on this world . . . something that reminds us all that their caring, fortitude and indomitable spirit has left this world a better place for us all.

A few years ago, I attended a women's conference of the International Organization of Women in Fire and Emergency Services, called I-Women, and heard speakers talk about women firefighters who have made significant contributions to the fire service and the respect they earned for all they had achieved. These women had been on the front lines of change and had stood firm in their resolve to make a difference. As a result, the women in the room, myself included, were honored to have been a part of that legacy and recognized how we had all benefitted from the path those women forged with their struggles. They referred to these women as "sheroes." I liked that. It seemed to resonate deep in my womb. I pondered the women I had known or read about in history to see if one in particular stood out. Then, it came to me.

My "shero" is Rosa Parks.

I first heard about Rosa Parks in grade school as part of National Black History Month, when I watched a documentary about her life. At the time, I lacked the capacity to fully understand the impact one seemingly insignificant act of courage could have. By her defiance on December 1, 1955, in refusing to relinquish her seat to a white passenger and move to the back of the bus (which was a violation of the existing Jim Crow laws), Rosa Parks turned a page in American history. With a simple act of defiance, she created a firestorm.

I imagine her at the time, boarding the bus and moving down the aisle, doing exactly what was expected of her and taking her proper place, sliding into the seat directly behind the barrier (or marker) which separated the white passenger seats from the black ones. As the bus moved along, more passengers boarded, and soon there were more white passengers than there were seats in front of the marker. Therefore, the marker had to move to accommodate the extra white passengers. Can you imagine sitting there, on the bus, lost in your thoughts of the day ahead when suddenly you have someone yelling at you to move? They wanted her seat. Up to that point, she had been in her "proper" seat, when suddenly, James Blake, a Montgomery bus driver, began to yell at her and three other black passengers, "*Move to the back of the bus!*"

I can only imagine her resolve in that moment when she was told to move and she pondered the consequences of refusal. She sat there like a stone, and within a short period of time, law enforcement officers boarded the bus and arrested her. Four days later, she was tried, found guilty and fined $10 plus $4 in court costs. Rosa Parks appealed her conviction and formally challenged the legality of racial segregation. It was the pebble in the pond that eventually grew into a tsunami.

Her actions on that day sparked in Alabama the Montgomery Bus Boycott during which, for 361 days, 40,000 black passengers refused to ride the bus, some walking as far as 20 miles to and from work. The boycott financially crippled the city's transit system, and eventually the lawmakers conceded and ended the segregation. Sometimes, people don't see the light until they feel the heat. Although widely honored for her actions years later, it was not without consequences that day; she was fired from her job as a seamstress in a local department store.

Years later, in recalling the events of the day, Rosa Parks said, "When that white driver stepped back toward us, when he waved his hand and ordered us up and out of our seats, I felt a determination cover my body like a quilt on a winter night." Several months after her arrest, during a 1956 radio interview with Sydney Rogers in West Oakland, she was asked why she had decided not to vacate her bus seat. Parks said, "I had to know once and for all what rights I had as a human being and a citizen."

Rosa Parks' statement reminded me of something that Frederick Douglass (circa 1818 –1895), an American abolitionist, author, speaker, statesman, reformer and advocate for women's suffrage (the right to vote), said about 100 years earlier, "Find out just what any people will submit to, and you have the exact measure of the injustice and wrong which will be imposed on them." Frederick Douglass sought to embody three keys for success in life:

Believe in yourself
Take advantage of every opportunity
Use the power of spoken and written language to effect positive change for yourself and society.

Rosa Parks believed in herself, used the power of the spoken language, and took advantage of the right opportunity to effect change for herself and for society. Long after the burning embers of her decision had extinguished themselves, I am able to lean on her for support. In life, sometimes you have to take one for the team, just as she did. In the throes of such an ordeal, when you feel isolated and begin to question what you stand for, it helps to have a shero and/or a hero to look up to and model after. As a female in the fire service, I realized I wanted the same opportunities and quality of life in the workplace that the men enjoyed. As my career progressed, you might say that I was faced with a decision similar to that of Rosa Parks . . . finding out what measure of injustice *I* would submit to in my refusal to move to the back of any "*bus*" warped in inequality.

No snowflake in an avalanche ever feels responsible.

~Stanislaw Jerzy Lec
writer

Three years after I joined the fire department, during a visit with my parents to San Diego, I was walking along the beach with them enjoying the sea at dusk, watching the sunset at the ocean's edge. As we strolled along, we didn't really say much, which left me alone with my thoughts. Up to that point in my career with the fire service, I had kept my impressions, opinions, and fears about my future pretty much bottled up. It's funny how you can pretend you are fine until someone close to you genuinely expresses concern, and that evening my dad brought everything to the surface when he simply asked me, "So, tell me Gina, how's it *really* going?" It was as if somebody had popped a cork. I began to tell my mom and dad the trials and tribulations of life as a female firefighter, and about the subtle and sometimes overt discrimination I

25

had endured without saying anything because of the very real potential for retaliation. After listening to me recount my struggles, I remember both my mom and my dad suggesting I file a lawsuit.

As I chewed on the idea, I realized all the incidents I was describing fell into the he-said-she-said sort of category, which can be hard to prove and often lacks any real concrete evidence. At the time, I was smart enough to realize that complaining to the department would only make it worse, but naive enough to think that one day it would magically get better all on its own.

I can tell you that retaliation is alive and well in any organization which isn't vigilant in watching out for its people. It can be so subtle it almost seems ridiculous when you repeat the transgressions to someone else, but as someone who had to live through it every day, it begins to feel like sandpaper on the soul, especially when it comes from multiple sources. In this life, the people in our inner circle—those closest to us—have the geographic advantage of figuring out our weaknesses early on. They manage to see the chinks in the armor, which make us vulnerable to attack. I can only describe it as being similar to the zingers a spouse or sibling can render with a mere sideways glance, a disgusted look, a tongue click, eye roll, or a sarcastic comment.

At that point, in my time with the department, I was grieving. I was feeling a sense of loss from the dream of what I thought a career in the fire service was going to be like, as compared to the reality of what felt like a *bait and switch*, or like I neglected to read the fine print on the sales receipt.

On that summer evening in San Diego, as I continued down the beach with my parents, venturing to describe my tale of woe, I began to recognize the reality and totality of my situation. I wanted it to change, and yet, I felt conflicted. I knew I wanted to keep my job, but I also wanted to work in a reasonable environment. Life in the fire department had begun to feel like living in a dysfunctional family, and I knew I would be perceived as a traitor for airing their dirty laundry if I filed a lawsuit. My goal had always been to get along rather than to cause trouble. In retrospect, I realize that changing an organization's culture, which is comprised of attitudes, beliefs and values, is a huge task and should not be left to the novice. Woodrow Wilson summed it up best when he said, "If you want to make enemies, try to change something."

Once you see the glaring hole and point out an unfair labor practice or a violation of policy, procedure or law, you inadvertently put a HUGE target on your back; a target that attracts revenge to your corner like fans to a boxing match. Revenge generally implies actions undertaken by an individual or narrowly defined group of people, which is outside of the normal boundaries of judicial or ethical conduct. The goal of revenge usually consists of forcing the *perceived wrongdoer* to suffer the same or *greater* pain than that originally inflicted by them. This may not happen right away, but as Pierre Ambroise Francois Choderlos de Laclos

(1741-1803), who is often credited with the following phrase's invention, said, "La vengeance est un plat qui se mange froid." Roughly translated, it means, "Revenge is a dish best served cold." The more time that passes between submitting a complaint and any subsequent retaliatory act, the more difficult it is to legally show a nexus between the two. This is one reason why it is such a challenge to defend yourself against such actions.

Looking back, I understand the reason I remained quiet for so many years and didn't officially complain was because, on some level, I knew I would need more experience and time on the department to gather the strength and confidence to face the backlash, which would ultimately come. I had hoped to one day be promoted to a position where I could make an agency-wide difference, but given the present work environment, I had already deduced that supervising my male counterparts would be met with resistance. I had also learned that pointing out inequities between the men and women was akin to political suicide. Don't get me wrong, I had complained about lower-level stuff through the typical channels a few times and quickly learned by the agency's response—or lack thereof—that I did not have their support. In fact, after I complained to the agency's human resources department about an incident, which occurred related to my first pregnancy, I saw firsthand their inconsistency in applying policy to me versus my male counterparts. It became pretty clear that the department would not be receptive to any complaint I might have. Getting a fair shake would not be the order of business; the rules that applied to some were applied differently to others, or not at all, if you were one of the unlucky few. This continued long after my graduation from rookie school. Eventually, my issues with the department rose to a level where inaction and tolerance were no longer an option and I could not morally abstain from taking action.

In 1996, nine years after I joined the fire service, our department *still* did not have adequate bathroom facilities for both genders in about one-third of our fire stations. We still had an open dorm configuration where the firefighters and engineers (those who drove the fire and ladder trucks), slept. The stations with open dorms had one large bathroom for everyone to use with a master slide lock that a female could deploy to keep the men from walking in while she showered or used the facility. Based on the internal culture's expectations, the only time I used the slide lock was when I was showering; it was acceptable and somewhat expected that I would not lock the door simply when I had to go the bathroom.

The open bathroom had individual stalls along one side with a separate line of urinals on the opposite wall. It was not uncommon for us to be awakened from our sleep to respond to an emergency call at 2:00 a.m. In such cases, the men would leap to the urinals to evacuate before suiting up and I relegated to covering my eyes to pass by them to grab a modicum of privacy in one of the stalls.

Since I was not raised with brothers, this was probably more uncomfortable for me than it was perhaps for some of the other females. Nevertheless, there was no time for modesty and I didn't have a big enough bladder to hold it while responding to an emergency and experiencing every bump and pothole along the way. I did what I had to do to make things work.

Since I had to also sleep in the same dorm as the men, I slept in my T-shirt/bra and shorts wearing them under my turnout pants on calls so I wouldn't have to change my clothes when we got a late night call. The last thing I wanted to do was slow everyone up–that extra minute could mean the difference between saving a life or a home. Although I tried to maintain a modest stance, the men could have cared less about my response and vicinity. I used to joke that I knew every kind of male underwear there was!

In truth, there were some fun times living in the dorms; sometimes it felt like a slumber party–except with a bunch of men. We stayed up late and had some great talks about our lives, our fire adventures, and about the relationships we had with the people we cared about. With that in mind, it still would have been nice to have slept in more comfortable attire and have had the luxury of changing my clothes next to my bunk rather than inside of a bathroom stall. It's okay once in a while, but when you have to do it every shift, it gets old.

With seven years in the department and eligibility for a promotion to supervisor (captain), the agency provided candidates who sought the opportunity to practice their leadership skills the chance to "act" within higher ranks during various shifts. This "acting" provided individuals a chance to utilize what they had learned and gain some hands-on experience before they actually obtained the rank; this privilege was determined by one's time on the department, which was seven years of service (although this practice has since changed). Following the captain's exam, I was ranked 8th on the established eligibility list, and I was given priority to act as supervisor over others who were not yet ranked. My chances of promoting before the list expired was based on future retirements of more senior personnel, upcoming promotions, and new station openings–all of which created vacant positions.

In the fire service, you have the option to place a bid to work at the fire station of your choice, based on your seniority. Since I had not yet placed my bid, I was considered a *free agent*, which meant I could act as a captain in any of the fire stations fairly easily. And I acted a lot. I grabbed every opportunity I could to get the experience I needed to set myself up to be successful for the time when I actually did get promoted. One of the places where I acted as captain was at Station 16, which was similar in design to the open-dorm style stations. Because it was a larger station, there were two captains in command on every shift. The opportunity to work with a more seasoned and experienced professional was appealing and especially beneficial because I would have the opportunity to learn from someone whom I could also model myself after.

In the larger stations, it was standard for the fire captain(s) to have their own dorm and office space with a single-use bathroom attached, separate from the rank and file. The captain's quarters consisted of an office, which doubled as a dorm, comprised of two beds separated by a desk and a couple of file cabinets. The room was small, but it had a single-use private bathroom attached that was only accessible from the room itself. It was considered a benefit of rank to stay in the captain's quarters, and no one else but the captain's used the captain's bathroom. As an acting captain, I was given, by virtue of the Rules and Regulations, the authority and responsibility that went along with that role. That included sleeping in the captain's office. I worked a 5/6 (which means that I worked five 24-hour shifts out of nine days–one day on and one day off to allow for sleep), followed by six days off in a row. On that fateful day in 1996, I showed up at Station 16 to work my first shift as "actor" for the entire five consecutive shifts.

The first shift was uneventful and unremarkable. I heard no complaints about anything from the other captain or the firefighters. When I returned for a second shift, things were going well until about 4:00 p.m., when the battalion chief (who is the supervisor over several stations), telephoned and asked to speak to me. He said he wanted me to move back to the open dorm to sleep with the firefighters because he had received a complaint that it didn't "look right" to have a man and a woman sleeping alone together in the captain's dorm. I was stunned because absolutely nothing improper had occurred (or would occur), and yet, I was the one being moved to the other quarters. The chief wouldn't tell me who actually complained, but he seemed to be adamant the current situation might be ripe for rumor and innuendo.

I told the Chief I thought the decision to move me was partial towards the men, and it was discriminatory. I also told him that to move me would inadvertently undermine my authority and send the perception that I was not really in charge. Perception is a very big thing in any organization, and it's especially crucial in assuring subordinates will follow your command in an emergency situation. After a few minutes of discussion, I finally conceded, but I asked the chief to kindly first put his new procedure (which deviated from past practice) in writing. A brief silence ensued. He told me he would get back to me after he checked with the assistant chief. Well, I suppose that everyone has a boss—someone they are accountable to for their decisions. When he called me back about an hour later, he said the assistant chief had unfortunately gone home for the day and (apparently to err on the side of caution) I could stay in the captain's dorm. Then, a few hours later, I noticed the other captain moved *his* bed into the main dorm. At that point, I think he was somehow worried about his reputation. He was a married man and the rumors had already begun to fly! The next shift came about and there was still no resolution with regards to what to do with me by any authority. The *plan,* devised by the other captain (and maybe the battalion chief, I really don't know), was to move the other female firefighter into the captain's dorm alongside me, which sort of negated the privilege of being the acting captain. Each subsequent shift seemed to play out like a round of musical beds with me not knowing what was going on.

Of course, all of this might seem silly now, but allow me to provide you some context to put a face on my dilemma. There were just two women sitting on the promotional list and we were sitting at #8 and #9 for a captain's position (the other female was next on the list after me). If I was promoted, I would be the first female officer in our department's suppression history to make that rank. Many of the men (okay, most of them) were less than thrilled at the possibility of reporting to a female officer, and they had been *very* vocal in that regard. The undercurrent of discontent had gone neither unnoticed, nor unfelt. However, it was my personal feeling that if I allowed myself to be banished to the dorm, any authority I might have been granted with my acting captain's position would have evaporated, or at least been severely undermined.

It was obvious the department had not adequately prepared for the arrival of women to captains' status, and consequently, they did not have a game plan for how to handle such situations. More importantly, I felt if I relented, I would allow a precedent to be set that would do a disservice to my successors, leaving the women who followed me to take a virtual back seat and be treated differently than the men. It would be much harder to fix in the future and such a separation of sleeping privileges would put an invisible (but very real) division between the genders. Was I being stubborn? Yes, I probably was, but not without good reason.

It was important to me, as it is to anyone, that I be respected, not only as an individual, but also for my ability to be effective as a captain. I felt if I acquiesced on this point and moved back to the main dorm room, I would be putting a Band-Aid on a bigger problem—equality within the fire service. Like the pebble in the pond, I suspected the totality of the circumstances would eventually exceed the sum of the rippling parts, forcing the department to make some changes. Unfortunately, the changes did not come in the form I had hoped for . . .

When I arrived for my fourth shift at Station 16, I received a telephone call from our chief's aide informing me to report immediately to Station 23, a single-captain station, to finish out the last two shifts of the cycle. Moving me to a one-captain station might have seemed like a rather benign decision, perhaps even a win/win for everyone, but it wasn't. They still were not dealing with the problem; they had simply sent me away as you might send a pregnant teen to live with a distant aunt until her delivery date. Eventually, they had to recognize the undeniable fact that there is a new addition to the family.

Not being able to act as a captain at Station 16 (and others like it with more than one captain) had its disadvantages. Each fire station had its own unique character, advantages, and fire considerations. If I were restricted to being able to only work as a single captain at our smaller stations, I would be limited to bidding on and transferring to ones with only one captain position as well, thus eliminating our larger stations which comprised about a third of the stations we had at the time. It also precluded me from working with and learning from some of the more seasoned captains–something only available at those larger stations. In addition, there was a fiscal impact since there was a small stipend when acting to a higher classification and without the ability to work at any station, I would be limited. The edict handed down from the administration was now negatively affecting the availability of my options, and ultimately, my potential for professional growth. I realized I was at a crossroads, a point where I had to make a decision. It was then I decided to pick the hill on which I would later lose a lot of blood defending- I took my complaint to the next level. Looking back, I had absolutely no clue as to how much impact my decision to take a firm stance would have on the rest of my life.

I'm not quite sure why they call it human resources. It seems to me, when you think about it, they could reasonably call it *inhuman* resources. After all, the human resources (HR) department is funded by and designed to support the agency, which sponsors it. Similar to an attorney representing both the plaintiff and the defendant, it presents an obvious conflict of interest for HR to support both the department *and* the employee, even as it pertains to equal rights in the workplace. An HR department is only as empowered as their sponsoring agency allows them to be, and they can only be as effective as their commitment to stand firm for what is right.

Following the fateful day when I marched into the HR office and put my complaint in writing, I ventured into an abyss, which spanned the next 12 years of my life and included filing a grievance with the firefighters union, complaints to the Nevada Equal Rights Commission (NERC), the Equal Employment Opportunity Commission (EEOC), the Department of Justice (DOJ), and finally, Federal Court. I'm sorry to say that each of these steps was required and necessary in order to gain enough legal clout to get the fire department to sit up and take notice, and to ultimately gain some equal rights for women in the fire service. The decision to file a lawsuit against anyone or any organization should not be taken lightly as it becomes a living, breathing entity in and of itself and has the potential to suck the life out of your career, your energy, and sadly, your relationships.

While I was in the midst of all this, I continued to move up the eligibility list as vacancies occurred, and I was promoted to the rank of captain on June 6, 1996. This milestone in the fire service caught the eye of the media, as female supervisors were definitely a minority. At the time, there were four different fire departments in the greater Las Vegas valley and among them were only two other female captains valley wide. We had about 400 personnel at the time, so promoting the first female to the position of captain in our department was a big story to the local press. Internally, however, it was a very different story.

Now that I was in charge of a station, it became painfully obvious the men were less than thrilled about reporting to me. The resistance went beyond the subtle . . . it sometimes bordered on mutiny. Once, I had a male firefighter tell me, "We can make you look good, or we can make you look bad, and things aren't looking too good for you right now." The implied, *and often overt,* threats were very apparent, and, quite frankly, scary at times. During those first few years as a captain, I wasn't always certain that if I became trapped while fighting a fire that I would be rescued. It was a sobering reality and not a very pretty one. I'm certain my taking a stand about women's rights, along with the sleeping quarters issue several months earlier at Station 16, contributed to their general feeling of discontent and even mistrust of me. In reality, I didn't create the problems associated with integrating women into the fire service; I inherited them.

The other female sitting on the eligibility list was promoted a few weeks after me. In August of

1996, our Public Information Officer (PIO) called us both and asked if we would be willing to sit down with a local reporter and talk about our recent promotions. In an attempt to be helpful and agreeable, I conceded and allowed the PIO to give the newspaper reporter my home telephone number. She called the next day and when I informed the PIO of the day and time we were meeting, he told me he would *not* be attending. The reporter arrived at my home and interviewed me for over four hours during which I brought out my scrapbooks and excitedly shared my love for the profession. One question that came up during the interview (and one that I was frequently asked by others) was, *"How do you like working with all those men?"* I shared what I thought was a humorous story that occurred a few times in the fire station. I felt comfortable repeating it because almost every time I had previously shared it with friends and acquaintances, I'd gotten a giggle and/or comments like, "Well, boys will be boys!"

I went on to tell the reporter that during those first few months on the job, the men would sometimes pop in a porno tape during lunch break thinking it was funny and looking to get a rise out of me. At the tender age of 23, I blushed, covered my eyes, and embarrassed, retreated to the back of the fire station. The men thought it was hilarious. I soon realized, however, I would need to adopt a different stance or I would forever be banished to the dorm to sit alone. The next time they put a tape in, I stayed, and just after that cheesy music started up (*bow chicka bow-wow*) and the actor started unzipping his pants and lifting the actress's skirt, I asked, "Do you think the music is playing while they're doing this?" and, "How many people do you think are in the room while they're doing the filming?" I know they were stupid questions, but very embarrassing to the men who had to answer me when I was practically their daughters' age. It only took my doing this a couple of times before the videos stopped. We have definitely come a long way since those days, I'd say! As usual, when I shared this story with the reporter, she laughed, and I ended the interview by telling her I really liked the job and enjoyed the challenges. I left that day feeling really good about our time together. Who would have guessed the anecdotal story I shared would be captured in the newspaper article . . . just not quite the way I had told it to her.

Just before the article appeared, I went with my husband on a planned weekend trip alone in San Francisco, away from our four and six-year old children, which was a rare event between juggling fire shifts and family responsibilities. I had received word from the department that I would be given a temporary assignment as a captain in the training department as a cadre member for the upcoming rookie school/academy. I was feeling really excited and honored to be a part of that. Even today, I believe the experience of training those rookies was one of the greatest I had during my career in the fire service.

I got back into town late on the Sunday when my interview hit the newsstands. I made a beeline for the newspaper and hopped onto the couch in my favorite spot to read the article. I noticed right away that the writer blended the interview from the other female with mine as if we had shared experiences in the fire service. Aside from that, I felt the article was pretty decent and moderately truthful in its portrayal, although I would have changed a few things. Never in my wildest dreams would I have anticipated the nightmare, which was to unfold the next day when I returned to work.

I arrived Monday morning to the training division feeling enthusiastic and excited about my new challenge. I literally bounced into the office, anxious to get started and be a part of this new team. I got about two steps into the building when I literally felt like someone had sucked all of the oxygen out of the ventilation system. When you work as closely together as we do in the fire service, it's like a marriage, and tension has a way of taking on a life of its own. Everyone was acting strangely. I could tell whatever was causing it wasn't good and felt I was somehow responsible for it. I finally coerced one of the other cadre members into talking to me about it, to which he simply responded, "Read your emails." I felt like a deer in the headlights as a new reality struck me. I immediately went to my desk, booted up my computer and began to read a stream of e-mailed character assassinations, each one worse than the last. They just kept coming and coming. The threads were like a lynch mob screaming for nothing short of a hanging. Apparently, many of my colleagues had taken great offense to what I had been quoted as saying in the article. They were writing back and forth to each other and directing their emails to All Personnel, which included my supervisors as well as those outside our department, proclaiming that I should be disciplined and demoted. I was accused of embarrassing the department and they demanded retribution. At first, the emails were directed at both of us [females] because, although we had been independently interviewed, our comments were conjoined and intertwined in the article. But then the other woman wrote an email extricating herself and essentially disassociating any contributions which she had made from the more controversial parts of the article, presumably to take herself out of the fray, for which I can't really blame her. I felt stunned, embarrassed, hurt, and sad. Mostly, I felt incredibly alone. To make matters worse, the silence of the command staff transmitted a tacit approval of the comments made.

Not knowing where to turn, I called my HR representative. She told me the men simply needed a "forum to vent," and if I really didn't like it, I should send my own email. That advice seemed akin to throwing gasoline on a fire–it would only serve to make an already bad situation worse. Another reason I refused to write the email was because it would have violated the department's most emphasized rule in the Rules & Regulations related to the proper usage of the internal email system. The existing policy clearly stated the emails that I was being subjected to, and were being distributed by copy to 500 or so people inside and outside of the organization, were not acceptable and subject to disciplinary action. The last thing I needed was to give them any *real* ammunition with which to discipline me.

Would you believe that not one of the 17 individuals who used the email system, as a "forum to vent," were disciplined? When I recall the hurt and anger I felt back then, I think that it would have taken *only one* officer–a battalion chief or higher–to have sent *one* email, just *one*, stating that if my colleagues didn't stop, disciplinary action would follow. It might not have stopped the rumors, but it would have put a leash on the assaults and knocked the soapbox out from under my accusers. Because the management failed to address the situation, they made me fair game to whatever anyone wanted to write, without any consequences. In reality, the only thing I was guilty of was telling the truth. Allowing my colleagues the "forum to vent" wasn't healthy for the organization, and their written (and later verbal) attacks made my life a living hell.

During that time, I experienced hostility from my co-workers, hang-ups on my home phone, death threats, and total ostracism, which lasted for well over a year. To this day, I believe the reason management didn't respond and hold people accountable for violations of policy was because of the complaint I had filed months before about the sleeping situation at Station 16. Back then, they deemed I was not a "team player," and they were now letting me know it with neon lights.

Here I was, a new captain facing a lot of scrutiny and wanting desperately to fit in and do a good job, and no one . . . not one person in the department would even look at me. I would enter a room only to have my peers turn their backs on me and face the wall. I was told by the HR person that she was going to suggest that each time I went to a new station the battalion chiefs should call ahead to the crews I was to supervise and allow them to "opt out" if they didn't want to work with me. Her plan was that if someone expressed a concern or inability to work with me, the chief would allow them to request a transfer to another station during my shift–something that was completely unheard of in our department's history! Her suggestion sent me into a total panic! Thank God the command staff did not take her advice. It would have been a death sentence for me. Remember, I didn't do a desk job. Firefighting is dangerous work, and to do it safely requires an incredible amount of teamwork. For her to tell the crews I was working with that they had a *choice* about whether or not to work with me on their shift, she essentially was telling them they didn't have to listen to my commands during an emergency situation either. I hate to think of how my safety, and that of my crew's, could have been compromised had the department acted on her recommendation.

The months that followed the publishing of the article were by far the most difficult in my life. The unkind, rude, deceptive, and divisive things that people are capable of doing and saying is very disheartening. The tears started the moment I left work, and I cried in my car on the way home. I felt like I was wearing cement shoes under water. It took everything I had to find the energy to come back to work after my days off. What was worse was that I felt isolated in my pain. My husband was also a firefighter and suffered fallout for "sleeping with the enemy."

I have never been as close to suicide as I was during that time and yet, as dark as my life had become, I continued to work. One thing that kept me from taking my own life was working with those rookies in the training academy. For the next several months, they were my solace. I had 25 rookies who knew nothing about the situation and judged me solely on what I taught them. They saved me. While things improved over the following months, the situation didn't totally disappear. There are more stories I could share, and, situations of disparate treatment I was forced to endure that are almost too painful to recall. Suffice to say, if I knew then what I know now, that interview with the reporter would have gone quite differently. I would not have been so cavalier with my words in responding to her questions.

Sometimes I wonder how different my life would have been had I known what not to do in an interview with a reporter. But then, I realize we can't rewrite history . . . we can only learn from it and vow to do better in the future. C.S. Lewis once wrote, "Experience is a brutal teacher, but you learn. My God, do you learn." It's possible that everything happens for a reason, and as sad as those emails made me, they were the factual evidence and proof of the discrimination I tolerated that I later needed to show in court to keep my job.

Days after my interview was published and I sustained the e-mailed frontal attack, I numbly printed them all out and took them home, though I wasn't quite sure what to do with them. As I spread them out on my bed, I slowly re-read them, feeling the gut-wrenching impact of each one thrusting into me like a jagged knife. It was grueling, and when I finished, I collapsed onto the floor and succumbed to a river of tears. I truly felt as if my heart was breaking. I laid there like a puddle, wishing the world would stop turning on its axis, and it seemed like hours passed before I was able to move. I don't remember what shook me out of my self-induced coma, but I do recall that, on some level, I must have instinctively known some sort of action was required. If I did nothing, I would surely fade into obscurity. I had to do something about the emails, but what?

Like Rosa Parks, I was faced with the decision to either slink to the back of the bus or stand up for myself. I could have vanquished myself to obscurity or could I take a greater risk and embrace some of my greatest potential growth? It was then I asked myself the scariest question I could think . . . "Could it be me?" I knew that if I was to survive this ordeal, I would need to read between the lines to see what my colleagues were *really* saying in their barrage of words. Anger is never just about anger; it is about some other underlying frustration or fear. As raw as my feelings were, it was a challenge to try and look for what role I might have played in what led to this solitary confinement. I slowly began to put the emails into separate piles and realized there appeared to be a theme. The majority of them seemed to center around my not being a team player. I was accused of having gone rogue and acting like the Lone Ranger in trying to be the point man for my own agenda. It was hard to hear, and even harder to believe. I started to realize I asked the right question . . .

It didn't matter that I had suffered a thousand cuts and felt as if my soul was bleeding out. Resting on the laurels of "being right" put me smack dab into the victim role. If I ever wanted to recover, have the support of my staff one day, and be successful as a leader, I had to do something different from what I had been doing. However, their resentments ran deep. Winning all of them over seemed virtually impossible, so I had to develop an approach that was both sincere and effective. I decided to invest in changing people's minds, one at a time.

While I was engaged in the process of *really* absorbing the messages embedded in the e-mails and understanding the intent of those who wrote them, I was particularly grateful to a handful of men on the department who approached me shortly thereafter to ask me personally about "my side of the story." Given this opportunity, I was honest and forthright in explaining how the interview really went down. I learned that what triggered the drastic reaction of my fellow firefighters was the article's reference to the porno flicks that they presumably watched while on duty. The reporter inaccurately reported that I had said, "Their most favored viewing," which gave the impression they had a library of pornography, which they favored over watching, say, "Jeopardy." Although they were less resentful after hearing my side, they scolded me for being careless in the interview and giving her the literary ammunition to hurt the department's image. All said and done, if given a second chance, I would not have given the interview. It served no purpose other than to be a catalyst to humble me as I hit rock bottom, which is sometimes necessary for any true self-reflection. Since that time, I have been much more guarded during media interviews and I know that nothing is "off the record."

In retrospect, I believe if my situation had not reared its ugly head back then, a similar one would have eventually occurred in some other place involving perhaps another woman on the department. At that time, resentment over having women in the fire service was too prevalent, and it was bubbling like a simmering volcano waiting to erupt. Unfortunately, the consequences lingered on with the first crew assigned to me (after I left my cadre position I had during the rookie school), as they did everything short of insubordination to make my life miserable and, ultimately, sabotage my success as their captain. Luckily, I had a battalion chief who was willing to support me if I needed to do some paperwork towards progressive discipline.

Fortunately, before it came to that, I got my bid to a permanent station. It was there where I finally settled down into being a captain with my own crew. They gave me a fair chance to be their officer, and for that I am forever thankful. I grew a lot in the years, which followed, and it was with them that I began to believe in myself again, and in the department. I gained the confidence I needed to move forward and succeed. Nine years later, in 2004, I tested for the next rank and was subsequently promoted to battalion chief.

Now, when I look back on the months that followed the interview, there is only a remnant of sadness about the lack of support from some of the command staff who I knew to be men of honor. I suspect if just one of them had said, "Hell no, not on my watch," the retaliation I (and the other women) endured could have been averted. While I'm certain there was a great deal of risk associated with supporting a female under fire, especially from other females, true leadership stems from doing the right thing because it's simply the right thing to do. Supervision is not a popularity contest. But while I was stuck in the hallway between the door closing and the window opening, I learned that the true test of an effective leader is getting people to do what you want them to do, not because they have to do it, but because they want to do it *for you* based on the strength of your relationships. A relationship is like a bank account. You should make deposits for quite some time before you ever make a withdrawal. That way, when the inevitable bump in the road occurs, the trust has already been established and acts as an investment that will protect the relationship balance and give you a better chance of maintaining it. As a leader, I knew I needed to build trust with my team and as I began that process, I realized the first thing I needed to make was an investment in me.

SECTION 2

Emotional rollercoaster . . .

Ah yes, the past can hurt. But the way I see it, you can either run from it or learn from it.

~The Lion King
movie

Experience is not what happens to a man. It is what a man does with what happens to him.

~*Aldous Huxley*
English novelist

Confucius said, "A journey of a thousand miles begins with a single step." How true that is . . . and to add to it, each journey begins with a simple choice of which direction to go.

At some point in our lives, each of us comes to a fork in the road where we are torn between conflicting priorities. The decision of which road we take will ultimately shape the who we will become. As I entered the wide mouth of the road, I was often unaware of how narrow it would later become or that it would, in fact, define me. In speaking from my own experience today, as I stare at myself in the mirror, I am met with the wisdom that only comes from the privilege of looking backward in time. Upon reflection, I realize how judicious my choice was as I ventured down the path less traveled in filing a civil lawsuit. The path was lined with gravel and uncertainty. Yet, given the circumstances I faced at the time, filing a civil suit against the fire department was the only choice I had.

When I look back on the trials and tribulations I experienced, the real story for me was in something quite subtle. As I struggled to represent women's rights in the fire service, I was met with the conflict of figuring out who I was rather than simply what I stood for. The first concrete step in that process presented itself with the commitment to change the way I viewed people, places, and things.

Several years ago, when I first began snapping pictures as a hobby, I mostly photographed scenery. Occasionally, I also enjoyed taking a totally candid "gotcha" snapshot catching a friend or family member off guard. As I began to look through the scads of photos I had collected, I realized that, although the scenery was beautiful and, at the time, seemed to be the priority, the pictures with people in them ultimately captured my interest. Similarly, in life, the best memories seem to include the people we care about the most. Our careers can be paths, leading us through terrific scenery, and yet, it is important to take the time to build relationships that will last for a lifetime.

I can say from experience that when you decide to file a lawsuit, there is a prescribed path you must follow, albeit arduous and long, it is a path nonetheless. However, when we embark on finding our lives, the path is not as well marked and often we have to find it as we go along. I have heard it said, "The path is not even determined until your foot leaves the ground and is in motion for its next step." Now, that takes faith! It was in taking those first unsure and timid steps that I began to see what my character was made of. Ultimately, I graduated to confident strides, that is, until the road twisted and turned with new experiences and opportunities. In each new situation, I strove to find the balance between confidence and uncertainty and remain strong in my conviction to do the right thing. With each new beginning, there is also an ending. Children grow up, graduate from college, and move out to start their own lives; parents pass on, leaving you to become your own parent and thus, carry on the family name; and your career comes to a close, where retirement sends you into yet another phase of your life. Lawsuits, thankfully, eventually come to an end. With each ending, I added a few more drops of wisdom to my journey as I vowed to do it better next time, if it should ever occur again. The inevitable hurts experienced along the way seemed to fade and the personal growth gained brought a sense of peace that healed my soul.

We all have tragedies in our lives . . . things that rock our world and force us to decide whether to stand and fight or turn and run. The real question in any such situation is whether or not we embrace our humanness, including our weaknesses and vulnerabilities. Do we risk opening our hearts, even if it means we will bleed? Do we choose to believe in the wisdom of the human spirit and take comfort in it, even in our pain? Or, do we continue to put one foot in front of the other and take one more step, even though to do so is sheer uncertainty?

I will say this . . . being out there by yourself and fighting the good fight doesn't exactly put you at the top of the guest list for parties. Standing up for what you believe in can shake you to your core and leave you standing in right field all by yourself. Sometimes, it's in that isolation when you are forced to take a good hard look at yourself and with a critical eye, do what you need to do to stay proud of who you are. I must admit that during the loneliest times, I missed the friends who were not in my photos. It would have been much easier to just give up and reclaim my life, but I was already forever changed, and going back was not an option. In retrospect, the easier decision about which path to take was in filing the lawsuit and focusing on my career. The collateral damage was in losing precious time with friends and family and the strain it put on my relationships.

I remember very clearly the day I made the choice to sue my department, which was heartbreaking. There are many lessons I can share about that process and all that it entailed . . . such as the wisdom that comes from jumping into the deep end of the pool and *then* learning how to swim—it creates a learning curve you won't soon forget! Mostly, at the end of the day, when I look back on all the pictures of my life, I hope I will have more with people in them than mere scenery. However humbling life can be, when I look in the mirror, I want to make sure the person I face is one who stood up for what is right and true *and* proud of the fact that I stayed the course.

CHAPTER 6

Into the looking glass

No matter how long we have traveled on the wrong road, we can always turn around.

~Unknown

Have you ever heard that saying, "God doesn't give you more than you can handle?" Well, I'd like to add a caveat, "But sometimes He (or She) gives you *all* that you can!" God really likes to push the outside of the envelope and test our strengths and moral fiber. Regardless of what life sends our way, with every experience, we have choices. My husband and I brought both our sons up with the simple philosophy that in each situation in your life you have choices, and if you don't like one of them, choose another. Looking back, sometimes I wish I had taken my own advice.

There are times when I got so far into one way of thinking that I felt like I'd painted myself into a corner. I got stuck. Or worse, I got into a pattern of behavior that ultimately became isolating or self-destructive and I ended up replaying the same scenario over and over again, expecting a different result. I have felt the consequences of bad decisions, and in rising up from the ashes, I learned to accept responsibility for my part. In taking this first step, I began to take back some control and feel less like a victim. I also felt like I gained the upper hand in the ability to change my future.

Emotional pain is as real as physical pain and it can be debilitating and isolating. Sadly, some people can be absolutely brutal, inflicting callous and injurious remarks on others and leaving a path of destruction in their wake. Recovering from being the recipient of such an emotional attack is a process. At the time I was receiving angry and hurtful emails, emotionally I felt as unsupported as a trapeze artist swinging and flying through the air without a net. I wasn't grounded in my beliefs, didn't know who or what to place my trust in, wasn't grateful for anything, and I didn't have a plan. When we feel powerless, or aren't actively engaged, or feel we have no control over our future, it's easy to become apathetic, feel overwhelmed, and suffer significant personal distress. I have seen it many times etched in the faces of individuals at the emergencies to which I've responded.

On one particular occasion, I arrived on the scene of a 9-1-1 call for a suspected heart attack. As I entered the single-family dwelling with my crew, I was immediately bombarded with the stench of garbage. At that point in my life, I had never heard of, nor had I seen, the long-term effects of hoarding. I waded, knee deep, through piles of trash that included empty pizza boxes, old take-out containers, scads of unread newspapers, and what appeared to be worthless garage-sale items. I wondered how someone could fall so far into denial they couldn't see that they had a serious problem. Had they simply given up? I wondered if it happened slowly, or if it was the result of a life-changing setback. I don't understand the origins of hoarding, but I suspect it starts with the fear of facing a reality that is painful, and in succumbing to that fear, people relinquishes a part of themselves and eventually start *attracting* that very garbage into their lives.

I have flashed back upon that scene on more than one occasion and can't help but think some people are seriously afraid of self-reflection. They avoid the opportunity to really think about the choices they have made and how those choices got them to where they are today. A pool of water won't reflect unless it's absolutely still. I couldn't see what was really wrong when I was constantly in motion running away from myself, avoiding the truth, or worse yet, creating a false reality. Emotionally mature people are the ones who have learned to face the reality they've created and make responsible, informed, choices. The first thing I had to do was slow down so I could begin to look at what I had created and then begin the task of deciding which direction I really wanted to go.

It took some time for me to take a good, hard look at myself and come to terms with my role in the turmoil I was in. At first I wanted to scream at "them" and hurl every obscenity I could think of.

I wanted to throw all kinds of garbage at the situation. But really, where would that have taken me? I would have eventually become a bitter, resentful person. As Malachy McCourt aptly said, *"resentment is like taking a poison pill and waiting for the other person to die."* I was lucky I chose to change and take responsibility for my decisions so I didn't have to face a lifetime of health problems and ruined relationships, wondering why my life had passed me by with garbage building up inside.

Sharing my story is a part of my recovery. The key to rebuilding my life was to not give up before the miracle happened and to have faith that if I didn't quit on myself, it would get better. Faith is the act of believing the silver lining is real even though things may not get better, or happen, overnight. That day on the bed, with all those emails, I had to believe things would eventually get better and that suicide was not an option. In sifting through the wreckage, I had to clear the decks of clutter and reset my own expectations. I had to believe there was a silver lining to all that was happening around me.

There have only been a couple of times I really wanted something in my life and I didn't figure out, or have, what I desired–when what I was so sure I wanted just fell through my hands at the last minute crushing me and making me have to revaluate all I knew at the time. As I look back on those instances I realize I had a path to follow and those "losses" were a vital part of my learning and growth. It wasn't until later, sometimes years later, that I found the silver lining in not getting what I wanted, or thought I wanted, at the time. It is like the country song sung by Garth Brooks where he thanks God for unanswered prayers.

The first time I remember this happening was at the end of my first year of college. I had pledged Delta Delta Delta Sorority my first semester at the University of Nevada, Reno. During that first semester at college, I had gotten the prerequisite GPA required to become a full member, but because I had dropped a class, I did not make the minimum class credits and I missed it by one credit. All the girls that did not make the criteria that first semester were rolled over to the next and it was our hope to be initiated at the end of the following term, provided we met the requirements again. That second semester had been pretty good for me. I had made decent grades, or at least I thought, and most of my class averages were in the 80's and I was feeling confident I would be making the 2.2 grade average required to get into the sorority this time.

I couldn't believe when I got my grades, I had only made 2.0, just .2 short of the average I needed, I was in total shock! I was devastated. How could this happen? I never considered I wouldn't make it; I was crushed. When I went to my professors and asked them they said what I thought would be solid B's were actually C's because of the bell curve. My scores fell on it in relation to the rest of the class, something I hadn't factored in when I was happily going along thinking I was on solid ground. There was no moving any of my professors, and in one class, I had a 96% overall grade which resulted in a B because, according to the professor, above my average was the largest 'gap' so he decided to put the line there for determining A's and B's. It was not to be changed.

I left Reno that summer knowing I would not be going back. Not only was I crushed that I wouldn't get initiated, I was also humiliated and didn't want to run into my former sorority sisters and feel like a failure. I went home with my tail between my legs wondering how this could have happened. It would take years, a first failed marriage, and some life experience to answer why my dashed dream of being a Tri-Delt would actually turn out to have a silver lining.

As I look back now, I know that if I had made my grades, and gotten initiated into the sorority, my life would have been drastically different. I would not have become a firefighter; I would not have married and had the two boys I have now. Yes, my life would have taken a much different turn. Not to say it would have been better, just a different path, for sure. I sometimes think we get these *redirections* to keep us on our life path, to do the things we are destined to do and become. What initially started out as a failed plan ended up being a life changing new direction and one for which I am forever grateful in taking. I also realized if I had REALLY wanted to be in that sorority I should have studied harder and gotten all the facts. I tried to skate through on my inherent talents and had not really applied myself fully to my endeavor. It was a lesson learned that if I really did want something, I had to apply myself 100% and nothing less would be acceptable. It was a hard lesson and one I still feel the pang of regret over today. Even though I am very happy about how my life turned out I would have been very pleased to have been a Tri Delta too . . .

With that experience and knowing I held the key to my success (or failure) I looked at those printed out e-mails sprawled across my bed on that fateful day and I knew I had to make a choice. *Do I let this be the end, or a new beginning? Do I become a victim or a victor?* As I think back on Rosa Parks, she could have easily considered herself a victim, powerless over her circumstances, and willing to accept her lot in life. But she believed in her cause and chose to embrace the painful process of change. She saw the mountaintop of a different future and was willing to wade through the valley of its shadow to get there. Similarly, I also wanted a different future for myself and for all women in the fire service. I chose to hold true to what I knew to be right. Some of my loneliest, darkest hours have later turned into my greatest triumphs. And so, I began to conceptualize what the silver lining in this whole mess might look like. Next, I realized that *I* would have to change something; something I had not fully considered and contemplated during that fateful semester in college.

Changing ourselves is like cleaning out the hall closet–it gets messy and often gets worse before it gets better. Oh sure, I could have put it off, but eventually all that junk was going to come spilling out. Good or bad, it didn't get that way overnight; it was the result of a culmination of a number of smaller, daily decisions. A decision as simple as choosing how early to get up in the morning in order to get a jump on the day, or as complex as, "Whom do I marry?" The consequences of my choices ultimately summed up the quality of life I enjoyed. If I accepted I had created my own reality, then I could effectively position myself to change it. We have the inherent ability to turn a painful situation into a healing one simply by choosing a different attitude or a different perspective. That might involve accepting your part in the breakdown of communication. You might have to apologize to someone; or perhaps even more humbling, forgive that person for the way they treated you (whether they asked for it or not). It takes time to rebuild a life, but trust me, one day you wake up, look around, and realize you have a wonderful life, and you won't know exactly when it happened. That's the silver lining. That's when the pain of the past diminishes and your spirit is renewed with a sense of hope and promise.

Our perception of who we are, our beliefs about other people's motivations, and consequently the interactions we experience, can become clouded when our view is skewed because of our own inner clutter. Until I dealt with my emotional clutter, change and, ultimately, serenity would have been unlikely and I might have missed the silver lining that all of life has to offer and give.

The best time to plant an oak tree was 25 years ago. The second best time is today.

~James Carville
political consultant & actor

There have been several times when I have been in a really scary place. Rather than a physical location, the place I'm referring to is where I see myself as totally alone and emotionally isolated from my friends, family, and co-workers. I was too embarrassed to admit to anyone just how far below "happy" I had fallen, I felt misunderstood and afraid as life began to look incredibly bleak. Often, depression set in and I thought that life was against me. Life began to feel incredibly hopeless.

That's not a fun place to be. No one likes to be picked last for a team or pull the short stick. It's human nature to want to be wanted and needed, even if we don't actively ask for or reach for it. I saw this a lot in the fire department. A guy would start to be picked on by the other men and he would turn around and start to do the same thing to me, only worse. It was almost laughable to those around who caught on. The need to be better than "someone" is strong. No one likes to finish last if they can help it. Including me . . .

This concept was beautifully illustrated in the 2006 movie "Annapolis," where a first-year plebe at the U.S. Naval Academy (actor Jake Huard), whose character always seemed to be at the forefront of a negative spotlight, asked his roommate, Twins, *why* he hung out with him, given his low standing in the eyes of his superior officers. Twins responded, "People who live in Arkansas . . . you know what their favorite state is? It's Mississippi. Mississippi's the only thing that keeps Arkansas from being the worst state in the whole country."

"So I'm Mississippi?" asked Jake Huard.

Sometimes, people need to have a *Mississippi* take center stage so they can feel a little better about their own issues and when they don't, things can become very dicey in their thinking and lives.

At the time that I was filing my lawsuit, my home state of Nevada had the highest suicide rate in the United States (24.8 cases per 100,000 people). I learned there are five main risk factors associated with suicide:

> Sex/loss of an intimate relationship
> Occupation
> Depression
> Alcohol consumption
> Gun availability

Obviously, the more factors involved, the greater the risk. Unfortunately, suicide occurrence in public safety personnel is among the highest of any profession; partly because of the hours worked, the scenes witnessed daily, and the code of the silence encouraged by the profession. Sadly, during my career, at least three firefighters in our department alone succumbed to suicide that I know of personally. Having battled my own demons, I knew I was at a greater risk, if just by simply being in my chosen profession. Working on myself became a process I embraced with passion and commitment. I wanted a solid foundation to support my emotional health and buoy me along the way.

Suicidal thoughts were a wake-up call that I couldn't trust my own judgment and I needed an intervention. When suicide began to emerge as an alternative to the emotional pain I was in, I knew I mentally, and emotionally, had to "stop, drop and roll." Nothing–absolutely nothing–was worth taking my life over. No circumstance or person(s) deserved enough power to make me think that ending my life was the only way out. Suicide is a permanent solution to a temporary problem–I knew this. The only way out of such a dark place was to begin to share my feelings with someone I trusted. Many organizations have an Employee Assistance Hotline where there is instant access to trained therapists who can provide insight and a different perspective on whatever is causing so much pain. I know, it doesn't always seem like it, but trust me it *always* gets better. Whatever it is that feels so painful too shall pass. Sometimes, time alone was a great healer, but wasn't the time to *be alone* and isolated. As I look back, I wish I had done more about my anguish . . . much sooner.

Sometimes in firefighting, when we have a fire that is out of control, we have to take a really good look at the *total* picture, what can be saved and what is already lost. This is a process called "size-up." When a size-up is completed, we can better determine where to place our resources for the best results, to not only attack the problem, but also stop the loss and save what can be realistically saved. This size-up is planned and then executed methodically by professionals who understand how all the variables will affect the way the fire behaves. Similarly, when my life was out of my control, it was professionals who helped me "size-up" my situation, sift, sort, and come up with a plan of action to begin to turn things around. A good counselor or coach often uses cognitive-behavioral therapy–a process that engages our mind to see that our own thoughts cause our feelings and behaviors, and therefore, we are in control of our own actions. If some issue or happenstance keeps occurring over and over again, where we are the only constant among different players, there is a strong possibility it could be something *we're* doing, because we are the *only common denominator in our own life!* I realized I had control over my own behavior and how I chose to respond to situations in my life. Diving into and learning about why I did the things I did gave me a fresh perspective into my own nature and provided a new pathway to creating a better reality for myself. No solution can be formed in the same energy in which it was created. Therefore, discovery of whom I really was, what I truly believed, and how and why things had manifested thus far in my life, set up a new and different energy that would facilitate change. It's hard to complete that "life size-up" in front of a mirror by ourselves, because, let's face it, if we could have done it already, we would have! Somewhere we got off track and professional help can be the catalyst to get us back on the road to a better and happier life.

When my disaster of biblical proportions happened, I was in a state of transition in my personal life. I had two small children, with the oldest just starting kindergarten, I moved into a new home which my husband and I had spent two years building, and, I had just been promoted to captain. On the surface, life should have been great–but it wasn't. Following my shock over the response to my interview, I isolated myself. I didn't share my feelings with anyone. Instead, I isolated and tried to cope with the sadness, betrayal, disappointment, and fear, all by myself. I didn't trust anyone. After all, how could I? The mere mention of my name resulted in public displays of dissatisfaction. I ate my unhappiness, acted tougher than I was to show I was in control, and basically pretended I was okay for over four years. During that time, I gained 25 pounds. People don't always eat because they're hungry–sometimes it's to fill a void or comfort themselves in a way which provides instant gratification. We can only stuff those feelings down for so long, no matter whether we use food or some other thing to fill the void, until one day all of it begins to spill out. When it does, it probably won't be at the right time or place.

When it happened to me, it was on a Thursday. I was sitting at my desk in the captain's quarters going through some paperwork, working hard to concentrate in spite of the constant static buzz of sadness that had taken up residence in my head. I had tried for four years to compartmentalize my feelings so I could avoid feeling the sense of loss, which was my constant companion. On that particular day, my defenses were down and my thoughts wandered to all I had suffered over the last few years.

I felt a deep yearning and longing to belong. I watched the other firefighters high five each other, or talk about their camping trips, or nights out at the bar, always feeling like a fish in a bowl; seeing the people outside having fun but restrained within my small quarters. How I longed to be a part of that fun, to be in the know, to be part of those inside jokes and enjoy that feeling of camaraderie. Sure, they were nicer to me over the years and friendships were forged, but I certainly wasn't on the guest list for the overnight hunting trips. My gender alone made the firefighters wives put a kibosh on that idea. No, I always felt like the third man out, the wallflower, the little geeky sister no one wanted to hang around with but mom said they had to. Sadness wrapped around my soul like a misfit lifejacket that I couldn't seem to give up. It became my leaky life raft, dropping me lower and lower in the surf with each tide of memories my mind brought in.

That past pain recollected, my thoughts returned to the present as I attempted to complete my paperwork. The next thing I knew, I was experiencing chest pains. It started as a low throb and then my heart started to race with beats that didn't quite march in cadence. As I grabbed my chest and felt for my heartbeat I remember thinking, *This can't be happening. I'm only 36 years old. I'm too young to be having heart problems! This doesn't happen to people like me . . . this only happens to people who don't take care of themselves.* Beads of perspiration rolled down my face as I weighed the consequences of doing nothing against the embarrassment of a false alarm. I considered asking one of the paramedics to hook me up to a heart monitor but I was afraid of appearing weak. As a captain, and given that I was already in the "hot seat" with the department, I didn't want to give them any reason to suspect that I couldn't handle the job as well as a man. I couldn't let them see any cracks in my facade. Fortunately, within a few moments, the chest pains subsided and my heartbeats returned to normal.

With my training, I knew I should get medical attention, but like many classic heart patients I was in denial. Taking care of ourselves involves emotional care-taking as well. Following my own advice was a different story. I felt if I could take a "time out," and get away from all the daily stress, I would be able to sort things out. I must have sent up a one-liner prayer because within a few days, God responded. While I was hoisting myself up into our aerial truck, I suddenly felt an unfamiliar pop in my left shoulder. It was a torn rotator cuff, which in fire fighting translates to time on the bench. So much of our job involves upper-body strength that to be impaired is unsafe and gets you assigned to "light duty." The fire department *tried* to accommodate me and find a temporary job I could do that didn't involve strenuous activity but they were unsuccessful. Consequently, I was put on disability for five months. During that time, I began to recover from shoulder surgery, even more significantly, I began to heal my life.

That shoulder injury literally saved me, because once I was able to slow down and find a quiet spot in my life, I was given the opportunity to view my past hurts from a different perspective. I knew I needed to do something drastically different, as the energy soup I was sitting in wasn't healthy. Even if I didn't quite know the emotional cost I was paying, I certainly was becoming aware of the high price to my physical body. I needed help and I needed it fast. It was in my reaching out and finally asking for help that I was referred to, and began working with, a very skilled therapist. I also became involved with a support group. One of the most profound experiences during this time was in a seminar where the leader guided us through a "rage process." Before that experience, I was in so much denial I didn't have a clue just how angry and hurt I really was. Once my turn came around, I screamed so long and so loud I literally ended up with black eyes. In spite of the physical consequences, it was cathartic and I realized I had to pull back the dark curtain on my life and shine a light where I had been afraid to trek before. The payoff? I started to see the light at the end of the very long, dark tunnel in which I had been living. Suicide was no longer on the table as a last resort to the hurt I was feeling.

Therapy is like peeling back the layers of the onion, one at a time. They can't be ripped off all at once because it's too shocking to the conscious mind and can easily lead to more denial. As each of the layers was stripped away, it became okay to shed tears as I let go of another layer of anger, hurt, or pain. As I encountered life's hurts, I had inadvertently developed coping mechanisms and habits to help myself deal with the pain and other feelings. Although those behaviors may have served a purpose at one time, they ended up holding me back. If I didn't start to shed the short-term strategies I had developed to remain functional, they would have eventually become permanent character defects. I had to work to unlearn them as the unhealthy habits they had become. For me, my hesitance to let anyone see me sweat led to masking my feelings as my coping mechanism. I did not want to show I was vulnerable, or emotional, in any way because to do so while I was wading through the muck and the mire would have given my adversaries more fuel with which to attack me, or at least that was what I believed at the time. I had put in place response habits that kicked in automatically, regardless of the actual threat level. I thought my armor had so many chinks in it that I wasn't sure I would survive another full frontal assault, so I avoided contact with "the enemy" at all cost. Those automatic responses, which had once protected me, soon held me back from the very growth I needed in order to start healing in my life from the inside out.

The most disturbing thing about pranks, hazing, or social cruelty is that it is perpetuated (or tolerated) by those in leadership positions. One of the ways I was able to make sense of what happened to me was to vow it would never be tolerated under my command. Sometimes, I believe bad things happen to us so that we will ensure it won't happen to others. And that's exactly what I did for the people under my command. The key for me was to come out of my former place of fear, take back my power, and put myself in a position to stand up for what I believed was right. I made a personal and professional commitment that what happened to me would never happen to others on my watch as long as I had the ability and where-withal to do anything about it. You, too, can do the same for yourself and others. You have no idea of the impact you, as an individual, have on your co-workers, organization, or this world, for that matter. Your *caring* positively impacts all of those around you and makes it a better world for all. *You . . . me . . . we . . .* **are** the solution. We have to care, period. It was no longer okay for me to look the other way, to ignore the signs of discrimination or tolerate poor behavior; the stakes were too high, for the organization and me.

As I began to get better at sizing up situations in my life, I had to peel that layer of anger off which had been my calling card and really start looking at what was behind it. Was it hurt . . . pride . . . loneliness . . . ego? I had to become clear about my emotional health in order to take responsibility for my feelings. As my emotional health improved over time, I was able to see more possibilities and opportunities which were healthier and helped to prevent the discrimination I felt and experienced around me. I didn't want to die early from a heart attack because I was in too much fear of being my real, authentic self. I had to learn how to let it out, express it, and then, most importantly, let it go. I also had to make sure I didn't perpetuate it. It sucks to be discriminated against. It sucks to feel alone. Both are things within our ability to change. I needed to empower myself so I was part of my own solution. I would love never to see a suicide again; it's too tragic for everyone. Trust me, I've seen enough for a lifetime and for everyone it is heartbreaking, including the emergency workers.

If I could help prevent anyone else around me from experiencing that profound feeling of isolation, albeit from discrimination or life events, then I was onboard. It was time for me to get serious about changing and taking FULL responsibility for my role in healing my life.

CHAPTER 8

When life hands you a toilet brush...

I know for sure that what we dwell on is who we become.

~Oprah Winfrey
actress & philanthropist

At some point in our lives, we transition from being dependent on someone else to support us and tell us what to do, to being independent and responsible for the consequences of our own decisions. Making decisions takes courage, and making good decisions takes practice.

When I think back on my life so far and the times when I had a major life change, I had to look at what was going on with me at that point in time. Did I feel in control of the situation? Was I making conscious decisions? Or did I seem to simply react or perhaps fall victim to someone else's choices? I know I experienced each of these, on more than one occasion.

As I moved along the path created by me, it became important to be aware of my responses to what was happening around me. If I was feeling constantly down or feeling like a victim, or if it seemed like problems were appearing at every turn, then perhaps it was time to think about the rationale that went into each of the decisions and choices I was making. Life shouldn't be hard all the time. When I'm on the right course, life has focus and it is filled with optimism. The goal was to get to the point that I *liked* my life, which felt right and nurturing, and, like I was in charge. That doesn't necessarily mean I wouldn't experience some bumps along the way, but when they did happen, they wouldn't pull the rug out from under my world.

I've found, as I reflect back on some of the negative situations in my life, there were indicators earlier on which would have helped me avoid a lot of heartache if I had only taken notice of the message(s) being sent. When messages are ignored, they eventually become problems. If the forces in the universe can't get your attention with a problem placed in front of you, then suddenly you find yourself in the midst of a crisis.

No matter what career one chooses, it seems every industry, job, organization, or department has at least one superstar hotshot who the higher-ups revere as some sort of *golden child*. You know whom I'm talking about . . . that guy or gal who can do no wrong. Well, the fire service is no different in that regard and I can tell you it wasn't me. I really struggled during my first two years as a captain. I recall an incident that occurred at an apartment fire as I rolled up in our ladder truck (aerial apparatus). As directed by our protocol, I first approached the incident commander (IC), who happened to be our department's "superstar," and asked him where he wanted me to position the ladder truck to best fit his strategic objectives. I was surprised where he directed me to go and I remember thinking, *Are you serious?* His advice was obviously wrong and incongruent with any strategic consideration I had ever encountered. Just as I began to question his instructions, he barked, "Just get going and do your job!" Stunned by his attack, I silently turned on my heels, and, ignoring my better judgment, told my crew to set up the ladder truck as he had directed. I could see a few of my crew exchange glances among themselves, but they knew it wasn't up for negotiation.

Moments later, and within the eyesight of the incident commander, my crew began to extend the aerial ladder. Just as the water nozzle reached its limit, it became apparent to all that we were a few feet short of our intended target. The IC jumped on the radio and began to rant and berate me as being a fool for setting up the truck in that location. He purposefully and effectively gave the impression to everyone who was within earshot of the radio that I was an idiot and didn't know what I was doing. It suddenly occurred to me I had been set up for failure. As much as I wanted to scream something back at him on the radio,

I knew better, and instead, I calmly asked him where he would prefer we reposition the apparatus. He seemed to huff and puff and then, simply left us hanging without any new directive. The message he sent was, *If that's the best I can expect from you, then I'll just sideline you and work with someone who knows what they're doing.* Consequently, that ladder truck sat there unused for the remainder of the fire and my crew and I were assigned to other menial tasks.

In retrospect, the consequences of my unwillingness to push back was a message for me that I needed to be able to advocate for myself and stand up for what I knew was right. The damage he wrought that day on the radio with his dismissing and disgusted tone had a ripple effect in that my colleagues began following suit to imitate the same disrespectful behavior that our superstar had modeled. It seemed to be just one more in the series of a thousand cuts of the discrimination I was to experience, for what . . . I wasn't quite sure. It seemed that as a new captain I was not afforded the same opportunity to have a learning curve. My training experience seemed different than the men's in that any of my mistakes were highly publicized and amplified, whereas, my male counterparts were quietly pulled aside and corrected.

As I floundered, I tried to figure things out and learn my job in a way that kept me off the radar. My colleagues continued to isolate me with their often cruel remarks, antics, or rumors and a deep sadness set in because I had no one to confide in. I couldn't realistically complain to my battalion chief because it would just draw more attention to the fact that I wasn't fitting in. Besides, have you ever tried to explain the impact of a sarcastic comment or a roll of the eyes? Unless they're emotionally involved, most people just say, "Get over it and don't let it get to you." These are not the empowering statements they might be intended to be when you are in the midst of it.

After working side-by-side for several months with another captain who really seemed apathetic about me, he transferred out and a more seasoned captain, who I'll call Captain Heinrich Von Straus, joined me. Heinrich only stood five-foot, seven, but for some reason, to me, he always seemed much taller. Whenever he entered a room or worked a fire scene, his broad shoulders, rotund stance, and grandfatherly manner seemed to dissipate any tension that existed, and all those present felt like they were in the presence of a pro.

The day Heinrich arrived at my station, he entered the captain's quarters and found me on my knees, wearing a pair of rubber gloves, cleaning the toilet. He took one look at me and disapprovingly shook his head from side-to-side as if it just occurred to him that training me was going to be more work than he had anticipated. In my own defense, I proclaimed, "What?"

I could tell he was restraining himself. Carefully choosing his words, he responded, "If you're doing *their* job, then who's doing yours?"

Stupefied, I sat back on my heels, toilet brush in hand, unable to mouth a response. Perhaps there was more to being a captain than I had realized.

For the two years prior to Heinrich's arrival, I felt compelled to clean the captain's bathroom. I figured it was my space, only used by the captains, and it seemed unfair to make my crew clean something they didn't even use. I also might have been struggling with my natural tendency as a female to take care of my "nest." It never occurred to me at the time that I was potentially setting up the next female captain for unrealistic expectations from her crew. If *I* wasn't willing to act like a captain and focus my energy on the captain's primary responsibilities, then how could they possibly respect me?

Over the months that followed, Heinrich took me under his wing and began to show me the ropes. He helped me understand the political sensitivity within the fire department, when to speak up, and when to remain quiet. I began to learn that the higher you are promoted in an organization, the more important it is to build relationships with stakeholders. I remember feeling grateful and relieved to finally have someone who wanted to mentor me. His advice and encouragement were instrumental in helping me to evolve in my role as an officer.

Several months later, while we were in our office completing paperwork, a couple of the firefighters came in to clean the captain's bathroom. Guilt must have flashed across my face as Heinrich glanced over at me, and, as if reading my thoughts, he proclaimed a definitive, "No, it's not your responsibility. Stop feeling guilty." As I considered why I still held onto that connection to my past responsibilities, I realized I was trying to somehow stay involved in assisting the firefighters with their tasks so they would want me in their club and I could be "one of the guys." I felt if I had some connection to them, even if it was just cleaning toilets, my humble act of servitude would somehow translate into being a team player. In my head, it sounded something like, "*Wow, look at Gina, she's such a great leader . . . she leads by example. Those bathrooms are a shining example of how much she cares about us.*" It's almost laughable when I think about it now. What I realized under Heinrich's tutelage was that I was actually teaching them how to treat me, and by doing jobs they were normally assigned to do, I was saying I didn't deserve the same respect the other male supervisors commanded.

I didn't always catch the nuances of the early warning indicators (or messages) I was receiving, and thus I was not on the right path to fully realize my role as a leader in the fire service. My mentor clearly tried to convey I needed to establish boundaries and hold my people accountable. My efforts to clean the bathrooms represented more than I realized, and, I suspect it was linked to my natural tendency as a female to "people-please." I also viewed it as some kind of insurance policy with my crew in that, *If I'm really wonderful and helpful in every possible area, and I make your life a little easier, then maybe, just maybe, you might cut me some slack when*

I screw up. The absurdity of that was that I was trying to make deposits into some kind of emotional bank, but the problem was that I was putting my deposits and energy into the wrong bank. I lacked the confidence and know-how to realize that managing their performance and growing their leadership skills was what I needed to do to genuinely gain their respect. Instead, I was trying to be "liked."

Although I started to grasp the knowledge, skills, and abilities on one level, as the supervisor of my own crew, it seemed that when I was among the other captains and battalion chiefs (BC's) I slipped back into a familiar subservient role. I may not have been cleaning bathrooms for them but I was still intimidated and lacked the confidence to really contribute or exert my opinion during training workshops or at fire scenes. I felt like some of the more junior captains were surpassing me in the department's eyes. I knew I needed to change, but I couldn't seem to find my voice.

A new understanding came to me while I was working a house fire. I had received radio instructions from the battalion chief to direct my crew to push a leaning brick fireplace off a 2nd story roof so that, according to his assumptions, it would cease to be a threat. My better judgment and instincts were telling me that once this fireplace falls over, it was heavy enough that it was going to take stuff with it, possibly falling onto the people below and could even compromise the integrity of the roof for my crew. Even though every fiber of my being was telling me that my gut was right, I was still second-guessing myself as I thought, *Well, he must know something more than I do because he has all this experience, and he's the rock-star.* I turned to my guys and said, "I don't know if this is do-able, but let's just go take a look at it before we commit to it."

As my crew and I climbed the ladder up to the roof and balanced ourselves between the half-burnt rafters, I was confronted by the very real and present danger which existed, and I knew I was not being an advocate totally responsible for my crew's safety. Something snapped and I was suddenly a momma-bear looking out for her cubs with concern for nothing else. Right then and there, I gave the command, "We're out of here, abandon the roof!"

I've heard it said that you don't see the light, until you feel the heat . . . and that day I literally felt the heat. Afterward, I went up to the BC and said, "You knew that wasn't a safe roof and we never should have tried that maneuver." Based on my past experience, I fully expected to get blasted by him, but he simply shrugged his shoulders and said, "Alright." His response seemed so cavalier that, in that moment, I began to fully absorb the responsibility that came with my authority and I realized I needed to be more vigilant. That was a real turning point for me in letting go of my desire to people-please and taking command of my role as an officer. I felt a new sense of empowerment, which I had never experienced before. I was lucky my initial inability to question his command did not result in a crisis. Over the next few years, I could see myself changing, which ultimately changed the perception of those around me. I was letting go of the familiar safety of staying on the periphery and handling the props, and trading it off for the unfamiliar territory of taking command and being the go-to person. Over time, the negative interactions and false rumors I had been previously subjected to ceased. It seemed as I began to perceive myself more as a leader, those around me did as well. It all started with a new mindset- *mine.*

Changing can be unsettling and perhaps even painful because it requires us to look at how other people see us. The alternative, however, is staying exactly where we are and never growing in order to avoid facing the unknown, which is worse. We limit our options when we run away from change. As I've said before, we can't be successful in life unless we're first willing to be uncomfortable. Our ability to make the right decision rests largely on having the right perspective about the problem or issue. The hard part is getting the feedback that helps us find that right perspective. I was so lucky to have had Heinrich as a mentor. Finally, I had someone to show me a new perspective, a way of seeing the situation differently than I had before; for me that was crucial. I had been hitting a wall, doing the same thing over and over and expecting a different result. The bad thing is that it not only drives you crazy, it also beats you down. The more I tried to "please," the more I felt dejected and downtrodden and the more I went into a victim stance, which further lowered my self-esteem. It took the boost of self-confidence, which Heinrich provided, and the near miss at a fire scene that finally tipped the scales to make me do something different. I had to get really, really uncomfortable first . . .

As I contemplate my own life, I have found my problems have led to opportunities for my own personal growth. That personal growth experience would have been much less stressful if I had considered more possibilities while I was actually going through them. It would have been easier too. Why is it only after the fact that people can say, "Wow, that really turned out better than I thought it would." When we're in a victim role, it's too easy to fall off course. With the right perspective, life's not all bad, even if it does go off track from time to time. Famous telemarketer and author, Joseph Sugarman, once deemed "The Mail Order Maverick" by the *New York Times,* is skilled at using psychology to influence people by tapping into their emotional triggers. He summed up the purpose of keeping a positive perspective when he wrote, "Each problem has hidden in it an opportunity so powerful that it literally dwarfs the problem. The greatest success stories were created by people who recognized the problem and turned it into an opportunity." Throughout my fire career, people asked me why I stayed. It was because I loved to fight fires and help people. It wasn't always bad. In fact, there were some really great things about it and some great people there who gave me hope. It was that hope which kept me getting up after the kicks and made it worth the effort to find a solution. I desperately wanted to "fit-in" and be a good supervisor. I wanted to make it work and I knew if I could just "hang in there," it would. What I suffered from was lack of healthy relationships around me to support me through this process, both professionally and personally.

Life can be brutal in its unexpected twists and turns and sometimes, things don't turn out the way we plan them. We get hurt and become fragile when our emotions are in a state of turmoil. It's only natural to want to talk to others and perhaps spill some of the pain, sort of like releasing the steam on a pressure valve. In healthy relationships, our friends listen and support us, giving us enough space to work things out in a safe environment. This allows us to experience our feelings so we can move through them in a healthy way.

All too often, people who feel overwhelmed in a situation unconsciously create a drama triangle as a way to avoid facing their true feelings or taking responsibility for their own decisions. A drama triangle is where one gets pulled into an issue or conflict, hoping to gain support from another in an unhealthy relationship. There are three positions that are cast in such a mini-drama. There is the "victim," the bad guy (or girl) known as the "persecutor," and/or a third party who steps in to help, known as the "rescuer." Most or all of the *drama* in people's lives fits into one of these three categories.

The drama triangle was defined by psychologist, Steven B. Karpman, in 1968, and has been an essential element of inter-personal and corporate training every since. He sums it up the best with his description:

A **"Victim"** is someone who usually feels overwhelmed by their own sense of vulnerability, inadequacy or powerlessness, and does not take responsibility for themselves or their own power, and therefore, looks for a Rescuer to take care of them.

A **"Rescuer"** is someone who often does not own their own vulnerability and seeks instead to "rescue" those whom they see as vulnerable. At some point the Victim may feel let down by their Rescuer, or perhaps overwhelmed or even persecuted by them.

The position of **"Persecutor"** is synonymous with being tormenting or intimidating others. Often, persecutors are unaware of their power and influence, and frequently, exploit it in a negative or destructive way.

Victim

Rescuer   Persecutor

The victim doesn't look at solutions. Instead of facing their issue with maturity, they try to garnish sympathy with a, "Why is this happening to me?" mentality. The sympathy they receive temporarily numbs the pain, but unfortunately, pity doesn't solve the problems, it only suspends them there, like a puppet, stuck in their own story. I've heard it said that if you don't like your story, then rewrite it. It's easy to focus on the negative aspects of any story, because they can be far more dramatic and interesting to the listening ear. But ultimately, playing the victim will cause you to lose the respect of those around you. At some point, people begin to realize that you must be playing a part in your own victim story and they get tired of hearing it almost as much as you get tired of rehearsing it.

The victim shares their feelings and then, the other party wants to rescue them or fix the problem; or worse, they persecute the victim, accusing the victim of creating the problem in the first place. The rescuer feels they are truly "helping" and then wonder why they get hurt or shut out, never realizing that to be a rescuer, one has to see themselves as more capable than the victim themselves, which is not empowering for either. The persecutor has a great need to dominate and be recognized as superior and fears the loss of control, prestige, image, etc. In an effort to not be a victim themselves, they protect themselves from ever being one again, thus the "attack" of the victim. A viscous cycle ensues. Once that triangle is formed, it seems to take on a life of its own, and then, everyone is in for a ride. When people drop into these roles of victim, persecutor, and/or rescuer, there is no one to shut-off the music to indicate the ride is over and point them to the nearest exit. Eventually, everyone has to individually find his or her own way out.

When we get into playing these roles, we create a *story*. This story is a way to manage and control the players around us in the drama triangle. Everyone loves a good story; it makes us feel as though we are a part of something when it is used to connect us to each other. When a story is used to avoid and/or embellish our ability to be honest with our own feelings, it becomes a form of emotional black-mail, pulling people in, often against their will, so *we* get to feel or be something we believe we don't deserve, because if we did, we would have done it or gotten it already. It actually depletes the energy of all who participate, leaving them dissatisfied and wondering how they managed to get sucked in.

The problem is that we might initially receive the instant gratification of being the center of attention from such a fantastic story; but in the long run, if we are untruthful as to why we created it in the first place, it will eventually catch up to us. We'll lose the very credibility we once hoped the story would garnish as the fabric it was woven with begins to unravel. Those feelings we were avoiding, or not dealing with, will come to the surface for resolution.

Sometimes, it was hard to see where I was in *my story*, but here was my big clue . . . I could recite it in my sleep. It was well rehearsed and I could whip it out at a moment's notice to get some sympathy points in a conversation. The reason I created these "woe is me" stories is because I didn't want to look at the truth buried deep down inside, a truth that has disguised itself over time to cover the pain from which it originated. I seemed to always focus on the negative things that occurred in my life, because if I didn't have the drama, all I would have is a vacuum–a vortex of feelings to be avoided at all costs. It was that fear which kept the drama alive for me. I didn't want, or simply couldn't face, the fact that I played a role in creating the sad tale I told. It was easier to shift the blame to others than face the truth that I would need to look at in order to change how I really felt.

I must confess, when I was going through the discrimination and disparate treatment I received in my early days on the fire department, I got lost in the victim role. I bled all over my friends and family, telling them about all the atrocious things said and done to me. As I started healing, however, I was encouraged to take a different look at my "story," and uncover my part in it. Getting to the source of the pain sometimes requires you to unweave the strand of events in your life and retrace the steps that got you to where you are today. It's hard work to uncover shortcomings without placing all the blame on others. It's even harder to accept them.

In my case, I was a firefighter, in an almost all-male environment, fighting the system for a good and just cause. I had a mantra like Helen Reddy, "I am woman, hear me roar!" I speak from experience when I say I had an interesting and sensational tale of woe that garnered lots of attention and sympathy. It involved a colorful cast of characters, with a life and death backdrop, starring me as the leading lady cast into the victim role. I successfully made those around me—my supporters, family and friends—into my rescuers by capturing their attention, which further helped me to keep my story alive and well. The fire department, of course, played the role of the persecutor. I had it all! I was truly living and experiencing the drama triangle. Initially, it was much easier and more sensational to focus on what "they" were doing and the negative impact it had on me than it was for me to step up, draw a line, and express myself by saying, "No, I'm not comfortable with that." In order to recover, I had to change my life as well as my story.

As I started looking more closely at my circumstances, I realized I was contributing to the craziness, and instead of healing from the pain and moving on, I had become entrenched in it, and it was costing me greatly. Luckily, I saw the light before it caused a crisis and people were hurt, literally. The hardest part of pulling out of the drama triangle was to realize I played a part in it, and that ultimately, I could inflate or deflate it; the choice was mine. I admit I have struggled with going backward in time and revisiting the emotions and pain that brought me to where I am today, but I know its necessary to recount the details to provide an accurate portrayal of the totality of the circumstances. Ultimately, I don't want to be remembered for my victim story. In staying close to the truth and looking at the dynamics of each situation, I was able to discover my own blind zone and rise above it to reach my fullest potential.

The blind zone refers to a characteristic that others might be painfully aware of, but for some reason, you can't see it or the impact it has on those around you. Perhaps you interrupt others who are speaking because you feel that something you have to say is more important; or maybe you're perpetually late; or worse, you are inadvertently callous and insensitive in your effort to cut to the chase. Or like me, I had a need to people please. It doesn't always have to be negative, but those are generally the ones that get you in the most trouble. In my case, I cleaned toilets when it wasn't my responsibility. I've been told our blind zone accounts for only 20% of our life, yet runs about 80% of it. That means we interact with others and make choices everyday essentially unaware of the way we are communicating and the impact it has on those around us. We have all met people who drive us crazy for whatever reason, and we often think if they could just change one or two things then perhaps they would be better people because of it. Well folks, its not always that easy, because those things that need changing are often in their blind zone! In case you haven't realized it by now, everyone has a blind zone or two. Mine have played a few roles in my mini-dramas over the years, for sure!

Those closest to us can see our blind zones with great clarity. My husband once told me he saw my blind zone as a need to always be in charge. Ouch! Really? Here I thought I was just being a good leader. Case in point: A few years back, my family went on a vacation to Europe, and I became obsessed with maintaining control over everyone's passports. I was so obsessed that I held onto them until we reached each international checkpoint and then I stood there on the other side, like the Gestapo, waiting with my hand out so they could surrender them back to my safe custody. In my head, I was afraid of the consequences for everyone if someone lost theirs. What it boiled down to was my lack of trust and me "being in charge" was a result of that underlying behavior. Keeping everyone's passport helped me feel in control and safe. My blind zone was trusting, or my lack of it. Perhaps that behavior could be understandable with my 9 and 10-year old sons, but it really didn't go over too well with my 40-year old husband. Needless to say, my need to control created some strife between us, and eventually, our disagreement forced me to look at my motivations behind my behavior. I began to realize I was in a blind zone. With that knowledge, I was able to start making some modifications that better supported both of our needs in a more positive way.

Over time, I started to let go and trust those around me and I've been able to relinquish my need to *always* be in charge. In doing so, I am happy to report that people are a lot happier with me, too. But they couldn't show me my blind zone or make me change—that I had to come to on my own. The bottom line is that no one can change us; we have to want to change ourselves.

We seldom change our behavior until pain from the behavior outweighs the rewards we get from it. I've had to apply this principle in the workplace by allowing my crew the space and authority to practice making decisions and then supporting them in experiencing the natural consequences of those decisions. To stand in the way of that process would stunt their ability to take on more responsibility and grow as leaders themselves. In the process of letting go of my need to be responsible for everyone else's choices, to my surprise, I became much less anxious and a much better leader, wife, and parent. That ability to stand back and lead from behind made me more well rounded and balanced. No longer did I need to "prove" anything or "please" everyone. I just needed to support those I directed, and that was best done by expressing my expectations, which over time I came to know and embrace more fluently.

Sir Isaac Newton stated that an object in motion stays in motion unless acted on by an outside force. Unless you have an epiphany of sorts that rocks your foundation, you most likely will have a hard time getting a glimpse of your blind zone(s). In some ways, as I reflect back to my defining moment on that fire-weakened roof, I experienced an equal or greater force pushing me in another direction as I chose to protect my crew over being accepted by my superiors. I had an opportunity to finally see one of my blind zones with great clarity as my colleagues balanced themselves on those burnt rafters; I needed to start trusting me. Since my epiphany, as painful as it was, I've had the chance to discover one of my blind zones and work on minimizing its character defect.

Given my experience, I suggest you not wait until your world is crashing down around you before you recognize your blind zone. We all have strengths, but it's our limitations that keep us from reaching our fullest potential. If you don't already know what your blind zones are, then ask those around you. I assure you, they are likely quite aware of your quirks and foibles. If you're not comfortable with that, then I suggest you consider finding a group or a mentor who can help you identify your blind zones so you can start to move in a new direction. Just remember, when things around you are messed up and you continue to see patterns in your own behavior that generate negative outcomes, it's time to re-evaluate your perception of your life. You just might be in a blind zone. The longer you put this off, the more normal "it" will feel, and the harder it will be to muster the force needed to break free from your part in it and move on. Don't let your "story" become your reality. Don't let something that's easily changeable hold you back either. The most important thing I could do to avoid becoming a victim in my own life was to set personal goals and reasonable boundaries, to stand up for what was right, and learn to laugh at my own mistakes as I overcame my own blind zone. When life hands you a toilet brush—put it down and get busy!

Perhaps our eyes *need to be washed by our tears once in a while, so that we can see life with a clearer view again.*

~*Alex Tan*
author

Crying is a universal language, but are tears a vital form of expression, or simply the body's way of turning distress into a bodily function? I wanted to find out . . . Humanist and scientist, Tom Lutz, believes the ability to *not* cry can be attributed to learning to feel a different emotion than the triggering emotion. For example, I could choose to feel an emotion like anger instead of a triggering emotion of sadness, so no tears are shed. This ability to avoid crying may be handy in the workplace and other social settings, but studies show tears serve a very important purpose.

According to researchers, tears remove chemicals built up by the body during stress, which in turn helps reduce stress levels. The simple act of crying reduces our body's manganese levels. Manganese is a mineral that affects mood and is found in up to 30 times greater concentration in tears than in blood serum. Researchers found that emotional tears contain 24 per cent higher albumin protein concentration than tears caused by eye irritants. Maybe crying is more than just an "episode," actually something our body needs and is good for us? It was starting to look that way.

Further studies disclosed that one of the most important compounds eliminated through tears is *adrenocorticotrophic hormone* (ACTH), one of the most reliable indicators of stress. The researchers concluded that tears, which lowered stress, removed chemicals built up by the body during stress . . . Weeping, they conclude, is an excretory process, which removes toxic substances that normally build up during emotional stress. Conversely, suppressing tears increases stress levels and contributes to diseases aggravated by stress, such as high blood pressure, heart problems and peptic ulcers. This was starting to give a new meaning, and good reason, for a big cry now and then.

In a study published by biochemist, William Frey, entitled, *Crying: The Mystery of Tears,* he discovered that tear production might actually be a way to help a person deal with emotional problems. We've heard the expression, "To cry it out helps a person feel better," but how often have we also heard it said that, "Boys don't cry." From a young age, men are taught to associate (or disassociate) tears from emotion; women generally see crying more as a coping mechanism than men do. Scientific studies have found that after crying, people actually do feel better, both physically and physiologically—and they feel worse by suppressing their tears. These results beg the question, why are tears considered a sign of weakness when they clearly have such physiological and psychological value?

As a female trying to make a place for myself in such a male-dominated profession within the fire department, I felt it important I not portray any sign of weakness—such as tears—despite their reported probative value. I recall one situation, several years ago, when our fire personnel had to undergo our first in-service "diversity training." That was code for, "Don't do this or we could get sued." Back in the early 1990's, however, "diversity" was a relatively new term, and thus, based on the rather lame and uninformed annual training we were forced to endure; I can only speculate there wasn't much written on the subject at the time on women in firefighting. Our human resources (HR) representative who facilitated the class was quite uninformed about diversity. I can safely say that what she knew about diversity training and the challenges faced when both genders are working side-by-side in the fire service could be fit into a thimble. The group of about 20 individuals being trained during our first diversity workshop was comprised of firefighters, engineers, and captains (including me). The HR representative launched her training by trying to set the scene as to why women and men are inherently different and how that might spill over to the fire service. Unfortunately, the example she used went something like, "If your female captain starts crying at a fire scene, you need to ask her if they are 'happy tears or sad tears.'" I remember sitting there stunned, thinking, *What the f—!?! Are you serious?* Not only was she undermining the very essence of diversity training by using a minority to prove her point in a negative way, but she was also attaching to it a condescending annotation of her interpretation of what tears represented.

As you can imagine, as one of the only two female captains on the department and the only female student in the class, I was both embarrassed and offended by the insinuation that simply because I was female, I had a propensity to cry during an emergency response. I had never cried on a call, though I will admit that on some days when disparate treatment or a particular bad call had occurred, I was pushed to my limit, I had cried. But, I strived to never let them *see* me cry. I felt that if some of the men were to see me cry then I would appear weak. The HR rep's anecdotal example seemed to reinforce the fear that I would never be accepted as an equal and that women would continue to be stereotypically portrayed as "the red-headed weepy step-child" in the fire service, too weak and weepy to be equal to a man. To add insult to injury, since the derogatory comments were made by another woman considered to be an authority, it made such a scenario seem even more plausible to the men as they snickered and mimicked a woman sobbing while attempting to extinguish a fire. Instead of embarrassment, humiliation, or sadness, I felt a new level of anger start to bubble to the surface to cover my emotions. And thus, I began to attach a different emotion to my sadness so that it would not present itself in the form of tears. In the short-term, this coping mechanism may have helped me be tougher emotionally; however, in the longer term I believe it began to negatively impact my health and my relationships, as my emotional responses started to look like anger instead of what I was really feeling.

Since scientific studies have shown the cathartic value of tears, I concur when I say that in the long run and despite the bad rap that tears have received in our society, showing your emotions is really okay. Having emotions is a good thing—it means you are human and you have blood running through your veins. The key to sharing feelings is in finding the *right time*, the *right place*, and the *right person/people* with whom you can safely share. Crying is an excellent way to release stress and the toxins that can build up in your system. If, however, you find yourself crying a lot on the job, you might want to ask yourself, "What emotions are attached to these tears?" and, "Why am I giving this person, place, or thing so much power over me?" As I used these "safer" emotions to hide my hurt, I also displaced my true self and lost some perspective on who and what I was as an emotionally stable person in touch with my feelings.

There were occasions when I became so angry that I lost my objectivity and displayed a rather vis-

ceral response–tears might have been the safer avenue to take. One instance, in particular, occurred
when I was a senior firefighter with about five
years on the department. While I was attending
a required training with several other firefighters
and engineers, the captains who were facilitating
the class opened it up for discussion for the purpose of proactively identifying potential target fire
hazards in the community where special circumstances existed. In particular, there were some
apartment complexes that lacked easy street access,
which could translate into a delay in suppressing
a fire while firefighters put hoses and phantom
pumps (large diameter hoses used to bring the fire
hydrant water closer to the fire area) into place. To
understand how a fire grows, you need to understand what we call "the fire triangle." According
to fire triangle rules, in order for a fire to start, it
needs *fuel* (like a structure), *air*, and *heat*. Of those
three, the one element that firefighters have the
most control over is the ability to minimize or elimi-
nate the heat that is generated. To do so takes one
of the legs out from under the fire and makes it
possible to extinguish.

At the time I was attending this particular in-service training, I was in the midst of studying for both
the captain and engineer examinations, and in my
preparation, was conducting research about, and
studying, fire technology. I recalled one article in
particular which I had read in a trade journal that
was considered a "best practice" by a fire department back east, wherein they used five-gallon

misters (resembling bug sprayers) *first* when entering a burning structure so the steam created when
the sprayed water hit the heat (expanding it 1800
times) was the break needed to slow down the fire
progression, allowing the firefighters to put hoses
in place to actually extinguish it. Contrary to what
you might think, statistics show that most fires are
put out with five gallons of water or less.

As I shared this suggestion in the in-service
training that day, one particular engineer, who had
been my nemesis for the past three years, openly
attacked me in the classroom, accusing me of making up such a stupid idea. Given the fact that I was
the minority (in more ways than one), none of my
other crewmembers sided with me, because to do
so would clearly be social suicide amid their com-
rades. The scene immediately split the room and
opened the floodgates to create a platform for
those in attendance to air their repressed hostility toward me. It became an all-out sock-it-to-her
fest, completely out of proportion compared to my
seemingly innocuous suggestion of a five-gallon
spray bucket. The resentment I witnessed that day
ran much deeper than merely a difference in phi-
losophies related to fire science. This was the same
crew who, even years later, when they learned I
had bid to transfer to another fire station, put dog
feces on my bed and fish guts in my turnouts as my
"going away gift." Regrettably, I had endured their
abuse for five of the longest years of my life.

As the room turned on me like a pack of wolves,
the male captain facilitating the class told everyone

to take a break, and I left the room to retreat to a neutral corner. The next thing I knew, I was chest-butted against the wall, by the 6'1" tall veteran engineer who exemplified the term, "salty dog." He seemed to tower over my 5'5" frame as he blocked my retreat while screaming obscenities in my face, spitting as he did so. I somehow managed to garner a resolute stance that I didn't know I possessed. At some point, my fear that he was going to physically assault me gave way to anger, and then I refused to back down. Something snapped in me and in that moment, I became 10-feet tall as I gave it right back to him. I don't recall the exact words I used as I erupted and screamed a series of expletives back at his face, but the term, "stupid Neanderthal" comes to mind. As we both spewed forth our volcanic ash, spitting and screaming, I held my own as I emphasized my point each time with an accusatory finger towards his chest. He suddenly threw his hands up in the air, turned, and walked away proclaiming, "Whatever!"

And then, it was over. I stood there in a moment of stunned silence thinking, *Is that all it took to make him back down?* Suddenly, it dawned on me– sometimes the only thing a bully will respect is a bigger bully. I slowly walked down the hallway away from the remnants of the argument, feeling the eyes of my colleagues staring at me in stunned silence as they saw me take down their hero. It felt like I had suddenly developed courage under fire.

I didn't report the incident that occurred in the hallway that day, probably because I was not without fault in my response, but later, I realized I had changed in how I processed those emotional assaults and that anger had become my primary coping mechanism. I remember thinking that if anger was what it took to get their respect, then that was exactly what they would get. The ironic thing was that shortly after I transferred from that station, those same firefighters who argued so fervently against my suggestion to implement the water-sprayers as a first response in fire suppression, implemented those five-gallon water misters on each apparatus in their station. I guess it wasn't such a stupid idea, after all.

In the months and years, which followed, my newfound insight into the power of pushing back gave me strength and emotional endurance in other situations that occurred on the job. Each year, when I received my performance evaluation, I noted that the same negative boxes were always checked—as if someone had merely taken the prior year's evaluation and transferred over the information. Their criticisms fell into the more "subjective" criteria making it almost impossible to disprove them with facts. What was worse, the accusations weren't substantiated with any examples. My supervisor would write, "Gina is lacking upper body strength." As I read that I wondered, *How exactly was that determined? Was there some fire I was*

unable to fight as a result of a lack of strength? Or, was it simply because I was female and not as muscle-bound as the men? I resented the stereotypical negative feedback. My physical strength had never been an issue. I worked out regularly, lifted weights, and I certainly hoisted my share of fire hoses and equipment. As far as I was concerned, the criticisms were completely unfounded. I was tired of being on the defense and wondered if there was some way I could be more proactive to create a different outcome.

After reading the same comments over the years, I decided that the next year I would check in regularly with my supervisor and ask him what I could do to improve my performance in the hopes of receiving better, if not perfect, performance scores on my next evaluation. All year long, my supervisor always responded with, "Gina, you are doing a super job." I thought, *I've finally beaten it . . . I'm gonna have this one in the bag.*

Then, it came time for my annual performance evaluation. You can imagine my shock in seeing the exact-same gender-biased comments that had plagued me in past years and once again, made me look like a first-year rookie. I was at a crossroads. Would I play the victim one more time, or would I take action? Being the "nice girl" had gotten me nothing. Sitting on the sidelines and hoping my situation would magically resolve itself, or that someone . . . anyone . . . would get in touch with their humanity and see me as a contributor was really naive. In that moment, I realized that if I did nothing, then nothing would ever change. The same bubbling anger began to rise in my chest. It felt like my face was on fire. My anger began to overtake the sadness and fear that had kept me silent for so long. Well, I'd finally had enough. Each time I silently acquiesced, it only served to reinforce the power those documents had over me. At that point, I was a woman with nothing to lose. I had tamed the Neanderthal, so why not take on this evaluation issue? I decided to write a four-page, fact-based rebuttal to dispute my supervisor's unsubstantiated claims that I was not a team player, as well as his assertions that I couldn't carry my own weight in fighting fires. I placed my response in a sealed envelope in my supervisor's box and then, I waited. I waited for the axe to fall.

Days passed without a word. I began to wonder, *Did he read it?* Then fear started to take root and I began to second-guess my decision. *Had I overstepped my bounds? Were they going to try to aggressively "manage me out" of the organization?* It's hard to interpret silence; weeks of waiting for a response or action turned to months, and I began to figure nothing would ever change. But when it was time again for another performance evaluation, the outcome was quite a surprise there was nothing negative. As a matter of fact, from that day forward I got glowing performance evaluations. Was it because they had finally realized I was not going to roll over and accept it? It's possible . . . Some managers of organizations do that sometimes—they hope that if you feel unsupported, you will lack the confidence to speak up for yourself and in that powerless state, they can take advantage of you. If you're not careful, it could become your own downfall and lead to the loss of your job. Experience has taught me that often times, you don't get anything unless you ask for it, and sometimes, you have to get angry enough to speak up for what you know is right and refuse to be intimidated by a culture that punishes "complainers." It's not easy being a trailblazer in *any* profession.

The resentment of being the brunt of so many jokes and jabs over the years tainted my view of things, and I became sarcastic and outspoken with my disgruntled opinions. As you can imagine, sometimes as the pendulum swings, when we are learning to express a new emotion (like anger), it's easy to go a bit overboard. I didn't realize how angry I had become and how far my pendulum was swinging the other way. I have since learned that sarcasm is actually anger coming through really small cracks. Despite my newfound voice and resolute stance in speaking up for myself, it seemed somewhere along the line, I had unconsciously slipped into that role of playing the "victim" in my life. Indulging my anger without thinking through the consequences, or the aftermath, was something I later came to regret, as I began to acquire the reputation for being a "hothead" with a chip on my shoulder. Such displays of anger only serve to make others feel uncomfortable. It was hard for people to give me an honest response in the face of such anger, and the most accessible defense for them was to simply shut down and acquiesce. I knew I did *not* want to demonstrate that as my leadership style. I speak from experience when I say that if you are so angry that you may say something you won't be able to retract, it's best to retreat until you can find another time and place to appropriately vent some of that pent-up hostility. It was a hard lesson I had to learn. I should have found an unbiased friend to give me a new perspective on the situation. I shouldn't have swallowed my pain, anger, sadness, guilt or fear, as my feelings were not going to magically disappear. To do so would have likely caused them to re-emerge elsewhere, and at a time when I'd least expect or want it. Whatever you work hard to suppress, you will eventually emotionally express. No, I couldn't fool myself into thinking I wasn't bothered by it. When I read those e-mails from co-workers after my interview, I had to get very real with myself and recognize what people were saying about me was exposing me for what I was. In essence, it pulled my covers. All those emotions I thought I was suppressing were actually expressing themselves in other ways, and they were not the ways I wanted them expressed.

I also learned that I had leaned on my husband—a fellow firefighter—far more than I should have for emotional support, which was just not fair to him. While he was good at listening, it was simply asking too much of him to allow me to constantly unload my burdens at his feet. Unfortunately, when he didn't share my level of frustration, I was disappointed and even angry with him! It's a wonder our marriage made it intact through that period of our lives, and I'm surprised I didn't simply burn him out. He couldn't be my everything and quite frankly, I shouldn't have expected him to be.

As I began to change the way I saw myself, and how I chose to interact with others, I realized that the ideal and most mature way to deal with my emotions was to find a way to express them in the moment—without it being a messy job. I recommend that in any situation you always be yourself from the beginning. Sure, it can be risky, but people can spot a phony, which can be worse. When I tried to be something I wasn't by putting up walls or exchanging the emotion I was really feeling for another in an effort to mask it, people sensed my disingenuous front, and I lost their trust.

I started incorporating some of these new insights at a training class being taught by a couple of our Battalion Chiefs, popular with the troops. As the class portion completed and we moved to the question/answer section, the chiefs started to take questions from those raising their hands. As the chiefs went around, they addressed the firefighters and engineers by their first names and the captains they addressed as Captain such-n-such. We had been doing this for about 10 minutes when I raised my hand to ask a question. When the chief addressed me (I was a captain at the time), he

simply addressed me as Gina. Without really thinking, I corrected him by saying, "That's Captain
Hall," and then proceeded with my question. You
could hear a pin drop; there was a pause before he
continued with his answer. The next time I asked
a question, he addressed me as Captain Hall. It
was a risk. They were rock stars but I realized in
that moment if I didn't address the transgression,
it would have an unwanted ripple effect. I needed
to be seen as an officer, especially by these very
popular chiefs. It worked. By them recognizing me
and giving me the respect extended to other captains, I was elevated. It required me to be genuine
in my response, without bitterness or malice and
speak my simple truth. Although it was scary, it was
what I needed to do. That day I wasn't disingenuous with my feelings and I insisted I be treated with
due respect. The nice thing was I was able to do it
without it being a messy job.

§ § §

I learned so much, as I progressed through my
career, from my relationships *and* my mistakes. I
sometimes wish life came with an instruction man-
ual, but I realize I probably wouldn't have read it
anyway. As I look back at the 23-year-old version
of myself entering a male-dominated profession, I
wish I'd had the maturity and wisdom to prepare
for and respond to what was about to come. But
then, that would be unlikely, because maturity is

the accumulation of knowledge from life itself in an effort to have a greater understanding mentally or emotionally; and wisdom is having the ability to make sensible decisions and judgments based on that personal knowledge and experience. Most 23-year-olds haven't made enough mistakes from which they can draw such conclusions, and it's hard to be teachable when you think you already know everything.

If given the opportunity for a do-over, to say that I would have done things differently is an understatement. One occasion, which comes to mind, happened after I had been in the fire department for about two years. The fire station is like a family home in a many ways. And like family members, firefighters are also creatures of habit in that each of the crew had a regular seat at the dining table. When a crew member was on his or her days off, the replacement for that shift knew to stand by and wait to see which seat was available before sitting down. My station was no different; I too, had my assigned seat. After lunch each day, it was customary for the crew to clean up the kitchen, and each of us would pitch in by flipping our chairs upside down onto the table so someone could sweep the floor. As I turned over my chair, I saw on the bottom side was a very detailed drawing of a woman's vagina. Artistically speaking, the rendition was quite accurate and obviously took some time to draw considering the detail the sketch entailed. I was faced with this realistic, anatomically correct depiction of a woman's genitalia, and it felt like my face was suddenly on fire. As the only woman at that station (on all three platoons), there was absolutely no doubt in my mind who the drawing was intended for.

I remember the incident as if it were in slow motion . . . looking at it in shock, feeling their eyes on me awaiting a reaction, and just wanting to cry. It was so embarrassing just standing there with everyone watching to see what I would do. I reached into my junk pile of potential emotions and the only one I could muster was laughter, so I just laughed like it was no big deal. I laughed so that it would give the impression I was a part of the joke, rather than the brunt of it. And then, the only other response I could assemble was to be the dutiful good girl, and using my pen, I began to get rid of the evidence. I spent several minutes obscuring the detailed lines with scribbles and crazy eights in the hopes that it would forever erase it from the chair and also from my memory. To allow it to linger seemed to give it more power. Being called out like that seemed so unfair. I had passed the same academy and probation and fought the same fires. I had taken the same risks as they had. Why was I being made to feel like a second-class citizen? Was it simply because I had breasts and a vagina? Could it be that unfair? Sometimes, I felt like I sold myself out that day by not making a fuss, and not being honest about how that prank made me feel. At the time, I was in reaction-mode thinking, *Don't let them see they're getting to you. It will only make it worse, and for heaven's sake, don't cry!* In retrospect, I think that by *not* making my feelings known, it actually did make my situation worse.

It was bad enough that I felt betrayed by my fellow firefighters, but it was even worse that my supervisor, who was in the room and watched the whole chair-sketch situation go down, chose to do absolutely nothing. His silence spoke volumes to both my tormentors and me. I felt like an abandoned child with no one to advocate for me. The worst thing about my circumstances was the loneliness of it all. I knew that if I complained, I would be singled out and made to feel even more of a pariah. It seemed like my situation would never improve. In the midst of my grief, I dove further into my coping mechanisms that, while they helped me survive at the time, later manifested themselves as emotional baggage, which I would have to unpack and re-sort to learn a better, more honest way to portray my feelings.

Enduring such scrimmages began to wear me down over time, and I longed to be rescued. Based on how I felt, I probably should have cried that day. At least that would have shown them the depth of the hurt they had inflicted on me. I have no delusions of grandeur, thinking they would have sat up and taken notice, realizing the error of their ways. Sadly, that probably wouldn't have happened, even with my tears. Their behavior was out-of-line, and, definitely over the top in terms of disrespect, so much so that I keep replaying my humiliation in my mind, re-enacting the whole scene with the *woulda-coulda-shoulda* regrets, hoping for a different outcome. To passively allow my colleagues to exploit me that way, and enjoy humor at my expense, seemed to give them permission to continue. Knowing what I know now, I understand that if you catch transgressions and/or disrespect at the first level and deal with them right then and there, they are less likely to reoccur. If you sell yourself out just to keep the peace, at the end of the day, you only have yourself to blame.

As the years wore on, I realized that to survive, I needed to learn to advocate for myself in a more meaningful way. Having since that time gone through the experience of filing a lawsuit against my department, which included collecting factual, direct evidence to support my allegation of the disparate treatment, I definitely would have taken a different approach in my response to the drawing of a woman's vagina on my chair that day, and it would have involved a camera. Taking a snapshot of it would have gotten their attention. If I had reacted more and made more of a fuss, it would have at least spurned a discussion that would have transcended all three platoons (on all shifts) that could not have been ignored by my administrators. However, on that day I did nothing but cover my hurt with circles, scratches, and crazy eight's. Many more years passed before I had the perspective needed to really advocate for myself in a more meaningful, empowered way.

Within a few months of my transferring to another station, I learned I was pregnant with my first son, Joe, so the fire department placed me on light/non-hazardous duty. As the time I was to go on maternity leave drew near, my husband, Brent (both a firefighter *and* a paramedic), and I strategized how we could supplement the potential loss of wages during my time off. I wanted to save my vacation and sick leave for the time after the baby was born, so that I could spend time with my son or be available to stay home in case he got sick. I planned to work up until about ten days before my delivery due date.

Back in 1990, the fire department had a policy that allowed firefighters to trade or surrender shifts with other firefighters. Since Brent and I pooled our income as a couple, we decided to have him work my last ten shifts so we could leave some vacation time on my books and not experience any shortfall of wages. Although our plan was within the scope of the policy, it was unique in that typically the trade in shifts was reciprocal, whereas our plan would not require the *payback.* I had no intention of working ten of Brent's shifts *in trade.* When the administration received our request and figured out what we were doing, they refused to allow the trade to occur stating it was because he was a paramedic and I was not. Of course, I personally knew of several instances where it had been allowed for my male counterparts. I felt I was being discriminated against, and so, filed a grievance, which was subsequently denied. In response, I filed an appeal, which led to a scheduled meeting with the HR director. Knowing what I was up against, I felt like I was entering a bad neighborhood, and I didn't want to go in alone. I brought my mother along to be a witness and for moral support. Upon arrival, as we were being escorted into a conference room, I introduced my mother to the HR director simply as "Connie."

As the HR Director began to speak, he adopted a condescending demeanor and refused to make meaningful eye contact with either of us. If he intended to transmit that we were wasting his time, his message was coming through loud and clear. Nonetheless, I was determined to make my point and win my appeal with the hopes of receiving consideration while I was off on maternity leave.

There I sat, eight-months pregnant and frustrated, with tears threatening to slide down my cheeks and onto my shirt as he rambled on about how my request was against policy and procedure. It seemed obvious that nothing was going to come of this meeting and highly probable the letter of denial for my appeal was probably already typed and signed, waiting for the meeting to conclude. It was about that time that my mother, a rather unassuming woman who had been sitting quietly off to the side, addressed the HR director by name. He slowly responded by gradually turning his body in her direction in an exaggerated manner, followed by a disgusted roll of his eyes as if to say, "What could *you* possibly say that would make a difference?"

Now, it's important to note that back in 1990, there weren't very many women in positions of authority, or so they thought, and I think the HR director probably underestimated my mother, assuming her to be some sort of carpooling, stay-at-home, part-time room mother. He was totally unaware that she was actually a highly respected director for the county's school district, responsible for all the student disciplinary issues, expulsions and legal compliance necessary to avoid and mitigate any resulting litigation.

It was then I saw a side of my mom, which I had never seen before. I always knew she was intelligent, kind to everyone and could, with amazing recall, tell you every dessert she has ever eaten while on vacation. At that moment, as she straightened up in her chair, she seemed to grow to ten feet tall. In a legalistic manner, she took total command of the meeting as she stated, "Let me see if I understand you correctly." Then, she proceeded to provide a recap of the facts that were on the table, comparing them to existing policies and procedures, and then juxtaposing the conclusions to existing labor laws. I can tell you, when she was done, it did not portray the fire department's stance in a positive light. I felt myself fade into the background as my mother held the floor, and like a Philadelphia attorney, punched holes in his case.

I saw the HR director suddenly sit up straight in his seat and adjust his tie. He began to respond with, "Yes, ma'am," and, "No, ma'am." And just as suddenly, it became apparent that he knew, that she knew, that he knew she knew the department's decision wouldn't hold up in court. That day, as my mother advocated for me in a way I was not yet capable of doing for myself, I was both relieved and proud at the same time. I could see the look on the HR director's face as he tried to restrain himself from asking her, "What is it that you said you did for a living?"

The next day I received notification that my request had been approved.

From that episode, I learned that I was right in bringing my own representative to be a witness and speak on my behalf, and I would never again attempt such a meeting without one. No, the next meeting I had would definitely involve an attorney. As time went on, I got older and wiser, and I began to make more formal complaints about the incidents I endured, and consequently, the pranks, disrespect, and discrimination became less frequent and less personally intimidating; but the departmental transformation still took time. In fact, it took years. Although my colleagues' bad behavior was never outright admonished by the upper administration, it came to be less acceptable and more regulated as each person was held accountable for his own actions, if not by the department, then at least by me when I was concerned. Each year as we were required to undergo those ridiculous diversity training classes, I felt sad it took so long for them to come about and that so many females had to endure and individually deal with their own painful situations before the department sat up and started to take notice. More often than not, people don't change until it becomes more painful to *not* change than it is to do so. Too often large agencies or organizations don't change their practices until they are found liable with a lawsuit pending or have to pay out large sums of money.

Later, in 1996, with only nine years on the department, I filed my lawsuit essentially putting myself on the forefront of change. I grew stronger as a result of it and I began to learn the power in the word, "No," and I mean a definitive, "*NO*, I won't allow that." There is no wiggle room in the definitive NO and it served to put those around me on notice that their behavior was not acceptable. I learned that as long as I was still trying too hard to be "liked," and to be the good girl, the respect I sought would continue to take a back seat. My spending 15 minutes making crazy eight lines to obfuscate a drawing of a woman's crotch was never going to happen again. I finally drew the line, and my empowerment came in the realization that I had the power all along—I just had to get to the point where I was willing to take the risk, grab the brass ring of self-respect, and use that power. I wish it had come a bit sooner . . .

If there's one thing that I have learned, it's there are times when it's important to feel and express your true emotions so they will be real to you and you won't have to spend all the time I spent unraveling the past to get beyond them. I often felt the weight of the emotion all the way from my head to my toes, but I contained my grief and packaged it, adding yet another burden to my backpack which would ultimately weigh me down and inhibit my ability to deal with the next situation effectively.

Emotions are like pebbles; some are bigger and some are smaller. Every time we experience a significantly negative emotion, it's as if a pebble is thrown into our emotional backpack. If we are healthy, self-assured, and confident, the pebbles of emotions are kept fairly small and fall quickly through the hole at the bottom of our pack. There is a flow and we are in it; life seems smooth enough so the burdens we carry around are manageable. On the other hand, when we are out of our natural state of health and allowing stress to take its toll, those emotional pebbles are larger so they don't easily drop through the hole in the bottom of the pack. These burdens continue to gather and weigh down our backpack and even create a sometimes–literal pain in our neck. We begin to feel resentful from all the weight we carry around, and things that used to be workable. We suddenly become overwhelmed and stressed. Most of my stress was actually unreleased grief, disguised as stress. I was grief-stricken by the things, which happened to me. I felt I had lost some of myself by not displaying an honest reaction. On some particularly bad days, I inadvertently tossed some larger rocks and boulders into my pack. Each time, the hole seemed to get a little smaller, forcing me to hold onto all my resentment. I wish I had gotten angry, demanded some action and some relief from being in the negative spotlight simply because, as a female, I had somehow imposed myself into the boys' club.

It took time and patience to find a balance in what I was willing to accept from those around me. Basically, we teach people how to treat us. As we mature, we recognize our strengths and limitations more readily and find there is no need to cover them up or apologize for being who or what we are. In essence, we don't crave or need as much approval to be confident; it's inherent. We develop a healthy balance of knowing when to say no and when to keep our mouths shut. Unfortunately, I was a slow learner on the "mouth-shut" part of maturity but I have improved over the years, though I think some of my friends might still disagree. At least now, I am back in touch with my emotional self, tears are free to flow, and, those boulders are once again the size of pebbles. It's nice to be back and have the ability to have a water works show, when necessary. I'll take that mascara run and a lighter backpack anytime!

Be the best lil' firefighter you can be.

~Kathy England
lawyer

In 1996, the first time I sat down with my attorney at her office, she asked me, "Well, why don't you start at the beginning and tell me what's been going on?" As I started to recall the events of the past, my heart began to feel heavy, like a cumulonimbus cloud filling with moisture just before a storm. I had intended to give her a chronological overview of the facts of my case, but what started out as a "Reader's Digest" version of the story turned into a cathartic purging of emotional trauma which had spanned over a decade.

It was the first time I had ever told anyone the entire story. As I strung together vignettes of harassing and retaliatory acts, which had been imposed upon me, I realized that it probably sounded as if they had all occurred over a period of weeks rather than years. My attorney sat there quietly listening, absorbing, nodding, and taking notes; all the while, the tape recorder captured my words. I teared up, then cried, and at times, sobbed my way through the recollections of situations I would just as soon have forgotten. Unaware of the time, I finally said, "Well, I guess that's it." There was a long pause during which neither of us spoke. As she turned off the tape recorder, she simply uttered, "Wow." When I looked at the clock . . . three hours had passed.

As I began to gather my notes and documents together and get ready to leave, my attorney rendered a piece of advice. "Gina, from now on, you've got to be the best lil' firefighter you can be." I was stunned by her comment, and my first thought was, *You've got to be kidding! Haven't I been through enough?*

She must have read the reaction on my face as she began to provide her reasoning. "When you file a civil lawsuit," she said, "it puts both you and your department under the microscope of intense scrutiny. They will be watching your every move. I want you to think about what you really want to achieve by filing this lawsuit because you're going to have to be in it for the long haul." I didn't realize until much later just how prophetic and insightful her advice was. However, I really took it to heart. The last thing I wanted to do was put an even bigger target on my back. As for what I wanted to gain— I knew in my heart it wasn't about money—it was about bringing change. I wanted to make the fire department a more reasonable place for women to work.

I wanted facilities where female firefighters could use the bathroom without the fear of being walked in on. I wanted to be able to change my clothes without sharing a broom closet with three other women. I wanted turnouts, gloves and air tanks, which fit properly so I could do my job safely and securely. Most of all, I wanted to be treated with the same respect and decorum as the men.

Change is easy to talk about, but hard to bring about in a bureaucracy comprised of old school mentality and public funds. I can safely say that change was definitely met with resistance from my male-dominated command staff. As I was promoted from captain (where I was only one out of 100) to battalion chief (where I was one out of nine), I discovered that change is accomplished much faster as you move up the food chain, because you get a louder and more succinct voice.

I was lucky, in a way, joining the department when I did. In 1986, the Black Firefighters Association had just filed a lawsuit claiming unfair promotional practices. That case settled ten years later, in 1996, the same year I filed my lawsuit. As a result of their case, the department was under court order to hire an outside agency to conduct all promotional examinations. This was a really good thing! Prior to that, there were some obvious fraudulent practices going on that were not in *any* minority's best interest. During the time the Black Firefighter Association's case was working its way through the court system, the fire department's HR department had already begun to clean up its practices making their testing process more objective and fair. The Black Firefighters Association case also involved various forms of discrimination outside of the promotional process, which is probably why it settled for $600,000, split between all the individuals involved.

From a timing perspective, I benefitted from the Black Firefighters Association's struggles in gaining equality within the department, and for that they have my heartfelt thanks. Generally speaking, as one who has "taken one for the team," you are not thanked or appreciated for fighting the good fight, even by those who get to hang onto your coattails as they glide down the path that you had to claw and scratch to forge. Unfortunately, despite the fire department's experience and monetary settlement with the Black Firefighters Association, their sense of quiet indignation prevented them from considering arbitration for my lawsuit, which would have saved the county a lot of time and money—12 years worth to be exact. By the time my civil case settled, the paperwork filed filled an entire 10 x 15 foot office, three drawers high, and that was only on my side of the table.

There is a point of caution here and it is that *change often happens at glacial speed.* It is never recommended to bring about drastic change without allowing time for a corresponding shift in an organization's culture, and sometimes, that can take a generation to bring about. When I questioned why we did some things a certain way, I often heard, "Because that's the way we've always done it!" When the people who have that view are in positions of authority, it's important to allow them the time and a season to understand, buy into, and embrace any change so that it can be effectively managed without divisiveness. Yes, it's important to take baby steps.

As I think back about the changes the department underwent since my first day of rookie school, including making us rummage through the used volunteer firefighter's boots to try and find some, which would fit a smaller foot, I am thankful. Those boots created blisters or fell off walking up to fires. It was over a decade later before the department started offering boots that actually fit a woman's foot and performed as expected. The boots weren't the only challenge. I was the first one to request and receive a shorter turnout coat so that when I climbed ladders I didn't have to make my air-pack waist strap double as a belt, suspenders that didn't have buckles that rested over and on your breasts, and turnout pants that allowed for a rear end. These requests continued for several years eventually to include appropriately sized gloves, air packs, etc., and I don't even consider myself short or small!

Since I was fairly vocal in my complaints and suggestions, I was on the front edge of many of the changes that came about. Again, I had to take one for the team. When the department decided to replace the wooden ladders and aging hoses with aluminum ladders and synthetic hoses (something done just prior to my rookie school and subsequent employment), they blamed the expense on the women's inability to carry the heavier equipment.

We hadn't even completed rookie school yet! Whatever it took, the improvement in both weight and function benefitted everyone. Firefighters often suffer from bulging discs in their neck and back, torn rotator cuffs, knee injuries, and a host of other conditions that come about from lifting, pushing, pulling and dragging heavy equipment. I was diagnosed with a bulging disk in my neck and back, and as it turns out, it was partially caused by, or at least exacerbated by, the position where the air tanks fall on a female's back, due to our often smaller frames—a design flaw that I believe, would probably cease to be an issue, and be made even safer for both genders, if more women were on the design side of the equation. Don't get me started on the testosterone-sized helmets! I cringe to think of the next generation of neck problems due to having a large helmet with a huge leather emblem held in place by a prominent brass eagle, not to mention the added weight of a portable light and door chocks. Granted, it looks cool but adds nothing to the function of the helmet. The weight it adds and the potential to injure the user's neck over time is not worth the "cool" look it provides. Sometimes a little perspective would be advised. If speaking up would protect our health, then I think it was well worth the effort.

It was definitely a struggle to be asking, begging, and pleading for things, which others took for granted, and then, when it arrived, being blamed, begrudged, and ridiculed for getting it. It felt like a revolving door of rejection, elation, and then rejection again as I got verbally beat up, sometimes just for asking. In fire department culture, compliments and positive reinforcement from management were scarce. I had been fighting fires in the department for about four years before a captain ever told me I did a good job. It was a Kodak moment, for sure. The expression on my face as I stood there was stunned amazement, like someone had just told me I'd won the Miss America pageant. I was so touched, I cried . . . and then later, I was "talked to" for being a crybaby. It was a no-win situation.

As I gained seniority from my time with the department, my situation gradually improved, albeit *very* gradually. When I became an engineer, my duties changed, and the "beat-up train" only pulled into the station intermittently as things seemed to settle down a bit. It was nice to be able to catch my breath and not be so "on guard" every moment. It felt like I lived in an alcoholic home, not quite sure what mood Dad was going to be in when he came home, leaving a get-out quick (emotional) bag by the window, lest things go downhill rapidly.

Once I made captain, I was the supervisor and got to set the tone at my own station. I no longer had to constantly be in reaction mode to those around me. As my crew began to get to know me, they learned the horrid rumors they had heard had very little validity, and most of them were downright lies. The men who stayed in my station often told me I was one of the best-kept secrets in the department. They seemed to appreciate my supervisory style; and why wouldn't they? I had walked a mile in their shoes, and I knew what worked, what didn't, and the value of treating people with dignity. I treated them with the respect they deserved and allowed them to have a voice in decisions that could be made democratically. A new generation began to evolve in the fire department—one of collaborative decision making. From a personal standpoint, I felt more free to be me—to allow my sense of humor to emerge and even have fun, which was very liberating after years of feeling like I had to constantly portray a cautious and vigilant persona.

As my life calmed down and I settled into my role as a captain, I was in a better position to be able to do something about the mistreatment of minorities, especially women. In addition, I had become more sophisticated in my responses to inequities, and my methods were more strategic and focused. This allowed the higher-ups to be more receptive as they digested my input. The respect given to me for holding a position that wore a gold badge came with the benefit of no longer being seen as the pain-in-the-ass that I once was. I sometimes saw the look on their faces as if to say, "Well, I guess a broken clock is right twice a day." As I gradually got their ear to recommended changes, I felt like I was growing as a leader in both their eyes and thoughts. I began to form more meaningful relationships with the stakeholders who held both the purse strings and the power. As such, I was privy to the larger challenges facing the department and the profession as a whole, and I was given the opportunity to proactively formulate possible solutions. I also found that change at the highest level was more complex than I had ever imagined and the consequences of error were much more severe, and yet, it enticed me.

One might think that in my newfound position as a captain, feeling like I was finally allowed to sit at the grown-ups table would have been enough to satisfy me, but it wasn't. I didn't want to simply be a participant and sit on the sidelines being the "best lil' firefighter," I wanted to be a decision maker. I turned all my efforts toward studying for the upcoming promotional exam for battalion chief. I wanted to have an even greater stake in the direction my department was moving and be a progressive player in the next generation of the fire service. And thus, another new chapter in my professional life began.

All the concepts about stepping out of your comfort zone mean nothing until you decide that your essential purpose, vision, and goals are more important then your self-imposed limitations.

~Robert White
author

The best part about becoming a battalion chief was that people started calling me back! Before, as a captain, when I called someone, depending on the person and subject, I might get an acknowledgement or an answer a couple of days later. However, as a battalion chief, my calls were returned almost immediately, or even better, they put me on hold and I was transferred to the person I wanted to talk to right away. At first, it was awesome, and then it was kind of scary because it became immediately clear, rank does have its privileges–scary because now, when I spurted out something, within an hour, it was being circulated as truth with the caveat that it came from "a battalion chief!" I went from being ignored to an authority overnight and the only thing that changed was the cross of two bugles on my chest badge. As much as I had studied and prepared myself intellectually, I had not realized the hidden benefits—or the consequences—of rank that were revealed only as you take that next step up the ladder.

Overnight, I went from commanded to commander. While I thoroughly enjoyed the responsibility and duties, I was a little slow catching on to the bigger political game in which I was now an active player. Within a week, I understood I needed to guard my impulsive remarks and think about whom I took into my confidence because the stakes were so much higher. I also realized I needed to be walking the talk if I expected it of a battalion of men and women. Integrity was no longer a concept; it was a way of life. As I went up in the organization, it did become lonelier. The rank of battalion chief was no different in that aspect. I was at the top of the food chain in the union rank and file and just below the administrative staff (nonunion 8-hour folks) upstairs. That meant we had to take the initiatives from upstairs and "sell" them to the troops downstairs, often creating conflict as it related to a long-standing policy or procedure. As it was, we were on the first rung of union grievances, usually filed as a result of change and since we handled the scheduling, we were always on the hot seat. People get *very* upset when you mess with their opportunity to make money, such as overtime, or vacation requests, or a host of other daily aspects of running a department with now over 700 personnel. It was a volatile position at times, trying to warn management of possible problems with their new policies or procedures, or convince the troops that the change that was upon them was a good one. I learned very quickly I wasn't going to be everyone's best friend. One thing that was difficult to learn was the "piss-off" pecking order: Who were my allies? Who did I soft shoe around? Who couldn't give a damn?

As in any other organization with more than one position, the fire service is deep in politics. Of course, I wanted to set my life up to minimize stress and do my job to the best of my ability, so I began plotting my own path to success. This meant I had to learn fast, get involved, and discover who the key players were. I also noticed very quickly that the fastest way to find out who those key people were was to get involved and not only at work. There's a saying: *If you want something done, give it to the busiest person you can find. They don't have time to waste and will get it done right away.* What's the best way to find them? Doing things where action is required.

It didn't take long for me to figure out that my biggest allies and best advocates were the secretaries and support staff. Although they answered to their bosses, they also had their fingers on the pulse of the department. Many times, they were instrumental in giving me the best information at the right time, and, more importantly, they also let me know when to steer clear of the bosses on a bad day. They became some of my best friends during my years as a battalion chief. Those were relationships I cultivated and cherished. They were able to teach me a lot about politics and how to negotiate a sometimes confusing system which made my life a whole bunch better. My favorites were payroll! They were able to keep me out of a whole lot of trouble by giving me a heads up on problems before they had a chance to be bigger mistakes. Yes, it was nice to have a few friends on the inside.

While those were relationships forged, I also realized I needed to continue on my campaign to win over trust one person at a time. My relationships in the department had become more stable but I was still in the process of fighting a lawsuit and that had its implications. Surprisingly, one of the biggest "fights" I had as a battalion chief was with another battalion chief. We didn't see eye to eye and when I got set-up yet again and pushed under the proverbial bus, I went to my supervisor, a deputy chief, to talk about the drama it was creating. As I was there, upset and hurt by his actions, my chief pointed out that no one wanted to be friends with someone who could sue them and I shouldn't be surprised by his attitude. I was devastated by his callous remarks. I managed to get out of his office and make it to the back staircase before I melted into a puddle of pure tears. While I was there sobbing, one of the secretaries on a break found me, sat down next to me, and put her hand on my shoulder, supporting me. I cried harder but it was nice to be given permission to feel the pain. When

I finished my hiccups of tears, she said some of the nicest things. I left that stairway feeling so much better because of her. Sometimes, people really are human angels.

There wasn't anything I could do about the lawsuit threat. It was there as part of a decision I had made nine years earlier. I had always strived not to be threatening nor to use the lawsuit as a bat to hit people over the head with, but it was there whether I wanted it to be or not. Since I was a fairly new battalion chief at that time and he was a new deputy chief, our relationship hadn't developed enough where he felt he could be honest and trust there wouldn't be a backlash onto him. I had to put more deposits into that trust bank before we could have a healthy working relationship. I had to get busy and show I was one he could, indeed, trust.

One way, in any organization, to get noticed and start building trust, is to get involved. That meant I had to find a way for me to shine and meet some of the movers and shakers around me. I realized, in short order, that standing in the back, not raising my hand, bitching, and not doing anything about it (like getting involved), simply didn't work, and it never had. Change is hard work; ask anyone who has had to do it a time or two. The question was, and in some ways has always been, "How?" How do I make my situation better and demonstrate leadership when the cards are stacked against me?

Now that I was a battalion chief, I didn't have the luxury of sitting on the fence. I had to embrace leadership and do it now. I had to start taking action, if for no other reason than my new position demanded it of me. It became very important to find people in the organization who were capable of getting things done. Like the saying, "It's not what you know . . . it's who you know." I needed to know those people. It was all about action. I had to be in the groove and have the latest information to stay informed and give the best information/advice I could to my troops. I didn't have the luxury of being lazy either. Taking action helped me up and out of my life rut; I didn't have time to be a victim to anything anymore. People were looking to me to make decisions and keep their lives safe. It was a tremendous honor and burden at the same time. It was one I didn't ever take lightly or without consideration. My life had definitely taken a new turn, quickly.

While doing some personal growth work at a conference, the woman running it told us something that really struck me. She said that how you leave your current job situation is what situation you will take into the next. I took that to heart considering how things were going for me at the fire department; I certainly didn't want to take discrimination with me. I didn't want to take this fight with me anywhere after the fire department –I had some changing to do, and fast! I knew instinctively that, whatever door fate brought me, I had to negotiate my way past it. If I attempted a different path that avoided the "lesson" to be learned, I would end up in front of that same door again and again until I learned to handle whatever "lesson" I had been trying to avoid. The goal was to figure out how to do it without the crash and burn. This is important because I realized with perfect clarity . . . *I WAS the only common denominator in all my relationships*! If I didn't like how things were going, I only had to look in the mirror to see what needed to be changed.

As I became more inspired, my persona changed, and life started to shift, not by big leaps and bounds, but in subtle hops and skips. It took time and it felt, at times, like I would take two steps forward, hear a comment, feel the heat of resentment, and be forced a step back. I always moved forward again, nevertheless. Each time I felt that hot poker of resentment, the words from that conference entered my mind and reminded me, *This is not what you want to take with you . . . the buck stops here.*

Getting involved helped . . . even if it was, or had to be, outside of my profession starting at a grassroots level. I was Vice-President of my son, Joe's, PTA during his 5th grade year at school and it was fun. I met more parents/teachers/staff in that one year than any other year he was in school. It was a lot of work, but worth it. I felt important, honored, and they were generally happy with my contribution; I felt the same about them.

Work was the same way–show them you care and they respond. This is where I got a great chance to win them over one person at a time as well. It can be hard to be heard in a crowd, a lot easier in small groups or individually. As a battalion chief, I became privy to information that was "blocking" the very thing I wanted for/from the organization, and I got to see it from a grander scale. One time a deputy chief gave me a great analogy. He said firefighters get to see things from the 100-foot level, captains from the 1,000-foot level, battalion chiefs from the 5,000-foot level and deputy chiefs at 10,000 feet and up. Their perspective is much greater; they see the entire landscape (problems/concerns) and, therefore, have a much better idea of how solving any situation is multifaceted. As I went up in rank, I became much more aware how "problems" were not always as easy to solve as I thought they were at the firefighter level. As my *vision* of the landscape from my higher level expanded, I became much less critical of those above me, and more willing to be a part of the system below.

Another interesting thing about me getting to the "big boy table" was *they* got refreshed on what the troops were thinking–even if it was just from a gender perspective offered by my presence. It was always popular to say that as people get promoted, they forget about the "little people." This is an important factor in teams; they should be diverse, in not only gender and ethnicity, but also rank as well. I do believe that after a time, it is easy to forget what impact decisions have for those on a lower level. When going full steam ahead, upper management can get too focused on the organization as a whole and not the people they serve. Having people involved from all levels of the organization gives the organization an opportunity to see from the "people's" viewpoint, top to bottom, and vice versa. When businesses stay conscious in their operations and are holistic in their approach to their employees *and* customers, they naturally embrace change and encourage leadership and thinking outside the box. These issues are sometimes lost when the bottom-line is involved and the pressure is on to get things done *right now*. Diverse teams are well worth the effort, and, in the long run save the organization more time and money than any short cut would offer without this valuable input.

So, how did I get involved at work? First, I started saying, *"Yes!,"* to opportunities that arose. I started in the areas I had complaints or concerns about first. I sought out committees and teams that were dealing with issues, which I had been passionate about and then got active in resolving them from the ground level up. I always felt if you were going to complain about something, you should be willing to get involved in fixing the problem. Some of those teams included the station redesign team(s), diversity, recruitment, turnouts, National Fire Academy Executive Fire Officer Program, I-Women, teaching at recruit academies, and developing programs, to name a few. There were some great paybacks for that work.

One thing I was pleasantly shocked about was an observation revealed after teaching a class in our recruit academies. I started doing a class on loss control, which is basically about how to do salvage and overhaul at fires. It was about a three-hour lecture that covered the basics and gave some insightful clues on how to do it properly and safely. I liked doing that class because I felt that 80% of firefighting is doing just that—salvage and overhaul—yet, it was given too little attention, in my opinion. I loved the class and after doing it eight times, I had perfected my lecture and enjoyed delivering the presentation. One of the hidden benefits of doing the class had nothing to do with the lecture itself; it happened when those new recruits came to my station after they finished their training. Those who had received my lecture had more respect, fought me less, and got along better with my crew than those from classes where I had not delivered the lecture. My theory? They saw me as a leader and an authority figure before they even graduated. Just this one class made a difference. Based on that experience, I believe it is vitally important to expose new recruits to minority teachers. It is their first introduction to an organization, and, having them see women and other minorities as informed, respected, lecturers, and teachers imprints on them that we are a force to be reckoned with; someone they should listen to. And here, I taught the class just because I liked it. There are always "unintended" consequences for the actions we take–this one happened to be a really good one.

Getting involved is one key. Taking on a leadership role was another. None of these things I did were done from the couch with a remote. It took sheer guts to walk into that room filled with all chiefs at the National Fire Academy in Emmitsburg, Maryland and feel worthy to be sitting there. It took tons of patience and negotiations when we were redesigning the fire stations to be more gender friendly. Trust me, there were more than a few times the TV remote would have been a welcomed friend! The first time, when, as a battalion chief, I had to tell a station to clean up the questionable magazines lying around, you would have thought Pepcon exploded again. Change is a dirt road, not the paved highway where those who follow later get to see and ride on. I had to hit the ruts, get chips on my paint, and endure a couple of flat tires, but the stories told at the end of that road are always more exciting than reruns! The trick was to remember the road of life is a journey and I input my own GPS coordinates. I had to put in the where I wanted to go. Where I ended up was based on the choices I made with each decision. I wish I had learned this earlier. I would have enjoyed the trip so much more and made better decisions along the way. When I got involved, I got more support for what I was passionate about and a platform to express myself; my decision making process improved as well as I narrowed in on the GPS coordinates that best fit me and my path. It can be fun traveling the road of life, so get involved and remember to pack a lunch–it's a long trip!

The difference between what we do and what we are capable of doing would suffice to solve most of the world's problems.

~Mahatma Gandhi
spiritual & political leader

If you file a lawsuit, guess what—you've become an advocate! And, if you are going to be an advocate, wear the title proudly. This was a hard role to step into when I was still feeling like I was being victimized. I wished I had embraced this earlier in my process. It took me a couple of years to really grasp this concept because I was too immersed in being a victim to my situation. This wasn't good for me, or the Fire Department, and it is not helpful for your department/business either.

So, just what is an advocate? In my opinion, it can be, or is, someone who is a pain-in-the-you-know-what for your organization, at times, or that "controversial" or headed-the-opposite-direction type of person. It is the person in the party who doesn't always agree with what is going on and

151

offers another opinion. I think a good example of an advocate is someone who offers really good solutions or support for situations or issues that others don't want to discuss or deal with. Advocacy is a learned talent and one I didn't come to naturally. I tended to piss them off first and then have to talk them into it afterwards–always a harder road to take. I envied those who could tap dance successfully through the land mines of judgment and prejudice.

I have learned from my observations that it is, indeed, true that the attitude of a department or organization is directly linked to those running it. If those at the top have sexist attitudes, it is tolerated throughout the organization and embraced as a character trait. You know, the monkey-see-monkey-do type thinking. If they are a tight ship, the same is true. People follow leadership, regardless of whether it is good and solid or weak and destructive. It gives us a sense of belonging to something bigger than we are—a community of sorts. We want to be a part of something bigger bad enough that unconsciously we may take on ideals we don't even agree with. Most of the time, people know when the culture in their workplace is wrong, yet, instead of questioning it, they just keep silent, maybe for the money, to keep the peace, or stay off the radar themselves. It is like a virus that permeates the whole environment, and, left untreated, gets larger and, in some ways, bigger than anyone ever intended.

I like to describe this conduct as *gateway* behavior. It is a behavior that starts out innocent enough and then grows without anyone being truly aware of it until it is too late. When I became a battalion chief, one of the first things I set out to do was to start observing the stations under my command. I started doing regular station tours, meeting with the captains, explaining what my priorities and expectations were. You know, standard stuff. I chose not to make any major changes immediately, but instead to observe first, and then weigh my first moves based on what I witnessed. This was partly because I was new, and partly because I was, as a woman, being watched. I didn't want a mutiny; I wanted compliance and I needed to get them comfortable with me first.

I spent the first month watching, observing, and getting my feet wet. One day, I went to one of my stations and they were all out on calls, so I sat down to wait for them. This gave me an opportunity to really look at the station and see it from a less official stance. As I sat there, I looked down and found strewn around the station day room lots of magazines. Many of them were, in my opinion, bordering on the inappropriate side of okay. I knew if push came to shove, the department would probably not back me in banning them. However, I felt they created not only an unpleasant look but also set a tolerance level that would allow much worse to creep in, if not addressed.

I waited until they got back from their runs and asked the captains to join me in their office for a meeting. That was when I brought the magazine situation to their attention. You can only imagine the uproar it created. *Here is this new WOMAN battalion chief and now she wants us to get rid of all our magazines! She is out-of-control!* The uproar rapidly spread from those captains to the station crew, and within a couple of days, the whole department. What nerve I had!

That day I didn't tell them why I wanted them to clean up and remove some of the magazines. I only told them to clean the day room up. I let the uproar, which I knew would come from years of experience in that environment, run its course. I also knew they would not listen to a word I said when they were upset. Some time had to pass before reason would come into play.

About a week later, I dropped back in and asked the captains into their office again where I explained to them why I had asked them to remove all the questionable magazines and cleanup their dayroom. It was then I explained "gateway behavior." I pointed out that what was happening was more and more questionable magazines were entering their environment, and without adequate vigilance, it would continue to spin out-of-control until it did become a serious problem. I told them I felt they had lost some perspective on the matter and I simply opened their eyes again. I asked them to look at the situation from the public's viewpoint and that of a female firefighter. It wasn't fair to the public to be exposed to such literature and clutter, nor was it fair to women firefighters to have to police the environment; that was the responsibility of the supervisors at the station. They needed to be vigilant and make sure they provided their employees a safe and secure working space. By not policing it, they opened themselves up to liability. I also explained that an un-monitored messy space was a problem waiting to happen. I would love to say they embraced the concept right then and there and said, "Thank you Chief Hall, you are the greatest!" It didn't happen. However, over the next four years as their supervisor, I never had to warn them about magazines again.

Now you might think, *So what? It's just a few magazines. Right?* Well, I started to notice a few other things about that station once my eyes were opened, and, really started looking. Not only was their environment in the station questionable, it extended past that. They would show up on fire calls not fully dressed in their turnouts. The monthly training hours required for each person at the station were not completed, and their skills at a fire were not up to my standards. Over the next month, I addressed the turnout issue, gave them a verbal warning on completing all their necessary training and basically, let them know I was watching them at fires and expected better performance. It took about a month for them to see I was serious, and then real change began to happen. I had fewer complaints about their crews, they came to fires prepared, and their training records became one of the best in my battalion. They started "noticing" themselves, becoming more aware, and it showed. The *gateway* gate had closed.

These were good men and they had a good crew. What was out of whack was they were operating from an internal viewpoint that had drifted away from the big picture. It took someone to remind them they had a part to play to make the big picture happen. In a lot of ways, this is advocacy. I saw a problem and I brought it to their attention. Once they were able to perceive the problem(s), change could start to creep in. An unintended consequence of what happened was that the word got out to the other stations I supervised and they started cleaning up their act without me even asking. They started to notice and wake up, too. I like to brag I had one of the best training records of any battalion in our department. I had almost zero disciplinary issues and I only wrote-up two people in my whole time as battalion chief. Some might say I had my head in the sand. I like to think I set a high bar and didn't overlook the little stuff that can become stumbling blocks down the road. I made the little stuff as important as the big stuff. If you can stop a problem before it happens—well, you don't have a problem. Do you?

This is the difference between leadership and fence sitting. One pitfall of fence sitting is complacency. I have seen businesses (and firefighters are no exception) get so bogged down in rules, regulations, and standard operating procedures that the only people who could possibly know them all are those studying for promotional exams. We've gotten so afraid to say, "No," to an employee for fear of being sued, we try to "legislate" all our behavior on paper. Over time, that mountain of paperwork ends up almost useless, until the hammer comes down, and by then, no one wins. If more organizations would empower leadership ideals, diverse thinkers, and multi-cultural organizational charts, some of this fear would fall away. It would be so much easier for the organization to address gateway behavior because the organization would be more sensitive and truly reflect the people it serves; it would become a natural part of the organizational culture. I didn't "do" anything crazy with the magazines; I didn't even ban them from viewing. I simply asked they be stowed away neatly and thinned out with an eye to public appeal and station harmony. The irony was, after they did this, along with cleaning up the other things too, that station actually worked better and seemed happier. It ended up being a good thing. Doing the right thing works. It didn't take rules and regulations or standard operating procedures. It just took a couple of bugles and caring.

▬ ▬ ▬

I always loved having someone on a committee who disagreed with everything we did. Most thought I was crazy, and sometimes, I did too! For awhile I served as Vice-President of the Firefighter Association, it was our committee's responsibility to manage and appropriate the $10 everyone on the fire department gave monthly that paid for cable, TV's, workout equipment, etc. Every time we discussed adding something new, one of our committee members would say, "No." A few of the members complained to me that we should remove him; he added time to our meetings and was argumentative. I told them I wanted him on because I knew when we made a decision, we were in integrity and had dotted our i's and crossed our t's. He made us consider every angle of the equation, so I felt secure when we took action that we were making the correct move, because, we had, indeed, covered everything. I hated when I was on committees and no one voiced an opinion—what a shame. That is why it is so important to be diverse in the organization and committees. We tend to agree with those "like us." Sometimes, having a little input from others, positive or negative, can change a whole concept, usually making it better than it ever would have been without it. I say, "Embrace advocacy!" Don't surround yourself with rear end kissers. I would rather have the occasional headache of having to explain myself than not consider all the angles. You might not like having that role on a committee, the one having questions, but trust me, you are probably the most valuable person they have in that room.

When an organization doesn't broaden its view, it can become a disaster waiting to happen. If an organization doesn't put plans into place, realize the impact they have, or take proactive steps to address them, an iceberg is likely to appear. As with an iceberg, what you see on the surface is often not a good representation of what is below, and caution should be exercised to avoid contact with it or disaster is likely to happen. Think Titanic! One simple way to address this is to have a staff that is diverse, and more importantly, have the diversity represented as a voice at the table. Most of the problems I inherited in the fire service were ones that, with planning on the part of the organization, could have been avoided. I use the word inherited on purpose. When you are in the first wave of "newness" in any organization, those growing pains fall into your lap, and it is up to you to help them "figure it out."

There's a saying, "some people dream of success . . . while others wake up and work hard at it." You may be the only person they hear on these issues, so make sure they hear a good version! Integrity is important, leadership is important, getting involved is important; taking on advocacy is a way to be heard in a meaningful context. You are it. Wear it proudly. Be that voice that needs to be heard.

CHAPTER 13

WORK is a 4-letter word

Change is never easy. You fight to hold on. You fight to let go.

~*The Wonder Years*
television show

If you really are committed to change, then there needs to be a willingness to work towards solutions. The operative word in that statement is WORK. I talked earlier about getting involved in various activities, committees, etc., as a way to be heard. One thing I found out quickly by being on committees was that change comes slowly. Just like turning an ocean liner, it takes time. It has been said, "Rome wasn't built in a day." Well, apparently neither are gender friendly bathroom facilities! Now, I can't speak for the private sector or other government agencies, but where I came from, it took patience and perseverance and the ability to hurry up and wait some more. I lost count of how many times they started a station redesign committee only to disband and begin again a year later. Now understand, we would make baby steps in progress. Every now and then, real innovation would come along and serious progress was made, albeit at a snail's pace. But it was progress, none-theless. My point is change requires persistence over time. Don't think you are going to be at one meeting or on one committee and the world will change. Granted, it could, but most likely, it will be an ongoing commitment to work towards change, one (maybe baby) step at a time.

I would love to tell you at the end of this yellow brick road of change, there will be a parade, your name in lights, people clapping their hands for all you've done and Oz will come out with a shiny new plaque commemorating all your hard work. Alas, that probably won't happen. By the time true change finally arrived in my situation, many, many people were involved. No one cared whose idea it was in the beginning. No one remembered it started as a result of a lawsuit being filed; fact was, no one really liked me all that much because I had been a "pain in the —." Well, you get the idea. I had to put my ego aside on many occasions and step back to look at the big picture. Was it important that Gina got a bathroom or was it more important to our department? There is a general maxim that a truly great leader is the one where, at the end of a great campaign, all the followers say, "Wow! Look what *we* accomplished." I had to get my ego to that 10,000-foot level and see the big picture. I'll admit it was hard at times. I felt I went through the wringer for that little piece of real estate and yet, no one said "good job" at the end. No one cared I had filed a lawsuit to get it—it wasn't about me. If you are in it to get your name on the door or accolades for all your hard work, I'm afraid I have to inform you that you might be very disappointed.

Luckily, for my ego, along the way I had some great examples of, and teachers on, how to let it go. One occasion was at the National Fire Academy in Emmitsburg, Maryland. I was there as part of the Executive Fire Officer Program in my second year of a four-year program. During the two-week stay on campus, I had a lot of good conversations with chiefs from all over our nation and around the world. One night, over a few beers at Ot's, the local pub, I got into a heated discussion about maternity leave with a small town chief. He had hired his first woman a couple of years previously, of which he was very proud. He had a department of ten full-time firefighters and a budget that barely covered the basics. He was in the squeeze that all depart-ments face, trying to keep the budget afloat in changing times.

He had asked me what I thought about mater-nity leave. In my boldest, hear-woman-roar bravado, I told him women should be granted maternity leave. I explained I thought she should be able to do office work during her pregnancy and be given time off after the birth of her child secure that her benefits and position were intact once she returned. I felt this was the safest and sanest way to handle pregnancies for woman firefighters and ensure the health of the mother and fetus. I was vocal in that aspect, saying men weren't asked to choose between a career and a family and, just because a firefighter was a woman, she shouldn't have to either. I told him that was the way we handled it in our department and I thought that went very well—a win/win for everyone.

After I got down from my soapbox, he posed a question to me: What was he supposed to do when she took off, as his budget only allotted for ten personnel, all of which he needed to run his town's fire department? He agreed that she shouldn't endanger herself and her unborn child, but he had a real-life dilemma in granting her time off without having the money to pay overtime for the nine-plus months she wouldn't be fighting fires. There was no way he could do that and still maintain the resources he needed. He was practically in tears. He didn't want to lose her as a firefighter but he really didn't have a solution for how to make it work either.

I have thought a lot since then about what he might have done, and I never really came up with a good solution for him either. His problem was not going to be easy to solve and he was going to need some input from a lot of sources, including that woman firefighter. It was going to be a big decision not only for that department, but also for that city. I did, from that conversation, realize that just because you want something doesn't mean it will happen. That doesn't necessarily mean it is because they don't want to give it to you, they may not know how. This is why it is so important to get involved. I hope he found a solution that was workable for all and she didn't have to choose between a career and a family. I also realized I had some real advantages being in a large metropolitan department, as not all departments have that same latitude. I became more sympathetic after that time and much more patient in my approach to seeking change. It's not always about what you want but what is best for all in the department, business, school, etc. There is a marriage of the two if you work together, and you can have the best of both worlds when you do.

The point is you have to *work* towards a solution; that wasn't always as easy as it seemed when I started out. Don't get frustrated when it takes a long time—stick with it. This is not a battle for the weary, and you should plan to be in it for the long haul. When things I had worked long and hard for started coming together, I had an amazing feeling of accomplishment. That was worth sticking around for!

CHAPTER 14

Getting out of my own way

For every problem there is a solution, which is simple, clean, and wrong.

~Henry Louis Mencken
journalist & satirist

Not all solutions are readily apparent—they require you think outside the box. There are basically three types of boxes–yours, theirs, and the organization's. I've found, surprisingly, that one of the hardest boxes to get out of has been my own! It required patience; it also meant I needed to see where my own biases were and how they were limiting me. I often found that by changing some of my limited thinking and patterns, many of my "problems" resolved both with others and the organization. Not that I became overly tolerant or anything, but I became more creative and cooperative. Therefore, solutions became more apparent and were easier to integrate. Sometimes, the best thing to do was get out of my own way.

One fundamental question I had to ask myself was, "How do I limit my thinking?" One thing I have taken with me from my time in the fire service is the ability to think *outside* the box. Every call we went on was different. Though some of the things were similar, in every situation the differences required adaptation each time. I became efficient at using my intuition and ability to see a number of possible solutions. With each experience, I was adding new "slides" to my memory bank. These slides helped me in adjusting to new experiences or more quickly to old ones. It was as if, based on my last experience, I already had some inside Intel on what was going on. This slide tray has expanded over time with experience and has helped me navigate better through life. That's why it's so important not to coast along but to embrace it.

Lack of slides can be limiting our experiences and thinking. I added a new slide during my conversation with the chief who was struggling with the maternity issue–some problems are not because "the man" was out to get me. Maybe he just doesn't have a good solution. I became even more aware that there are some issues not easily resolved. That was a big slide for me. It was easy to stay in a bubble of my own reality, insisting I was right, instead of challenging my beliefs against the backdrop of reality and seeing if they were true. Although I still strongly believe that being a woman firefighter should not be a deterrent to having a family, I do realize the solutions to solving how that looks within a particular department will take cooperation depending on where you live and work. My slide tray is much fuller today than it was in 1996 when I filed my lawsuit. That's why they say hindsight is 20/20. As we look back, we see it through all the slides we've gained and, therefore, all the peaks and valleys we would have avoided if they had been there before. However, what fun would there be in missing all the excitement of adding those slides?

Over the years I have had many men and women ask me for advice about promotional exams. In the fire service to be eligible for promotion, at least in the department where I was, you had to take a written exam followed in a couple of weeks by an evaluation at an assessment center. Most firefighters who were serious about passing this very demanding process would start studying several months before the test, sometimes even months before they knew when the actual test would be given. I started studying far in advance for the positions of engineer, captain, and battalion chief. The written test is pretty straight up, right out of the books and manuals selected for the rank you were competing for. You studied hard, memorized like crazy and hoped you got a great score (over 70% was considered passing). When you passed you moved on to the next level, the assessment center.

The evaluations at the assessment center are like a well-orchestrated dance. There are certain elements which must be prepared for in each phase of the evaluation. Some is based on technique, which can be taught, but a lot is based on your ability to think quickly and use your intuition, which can't be. Some of the elements you encounter are personnel problems, fire problems, and a writing exercise (the engineer test is slightly different since it isn't considered a management position), all pretty much industry standards. All the books give baseline knowledge on what is needed for the assessment center. In preparation for this assessment center, men and women would seek out veterans to help them study and hone their skills. I would get some of those people in front of me and be surprised they were only able to parrot verbatim what a book said but got lost in interpreting what it *meant*. They were at a loss as to the "why," which is the part that is gained from intuition. I would ask them, "Why did you implement it that way? Why did you discipline them that way? What was your reason for calling, or not calling, that resource?" And, more importantly, "How do you personally feel about this topic or policy and how would that effect your response to it?" As I started asking these questions, the house of cards would start falling. They didn't really know why they were doing it that way, because they really hadn't examined how they personally felt about it. It was what the book had suggested and it had sounded good to them. They were relying on rote memory and what others had told them about the subject or situation. What they needed to do was make it personal to them.

I don't blame them for that. I think "we" as the fire service did a lousy job of exposing them to other modes of thinking. Until the last few years, education was not a requirement for advancement so, like me, these people came into the department at 23 or so years old and their indoctrination into the fire service culture began. A decade later, when they started to promote for the rank of captain, our first supervisory level, all they could really bring to the table was the company line, which was sometimes a decade or more behind the business world outside and most of which was learned at the fire-house kitchen table. Now couple that with an imbalance in diversity and you can easily begin to see how the fire service could be culturally ten to twenty years behind the rest of the business community.

If students gave me enough time before the assessment center to prepare them, they received a reading list of non-fire department books to challenge their critical thinking abilities. This was designed to help them expand their toolbox of ideas and develop a more sophisticated response to common management principles and practices. I liked to challenge them to think about *why* they were doing things as much as how they personally felt regarding such matters, more so than how they would simply implement it. There are many ways to put out a house fire and handle personnel issues. *That* I know from 22+ years of firefighting experience. Why I would put out a fire in *that* particular way, with *that* particular tool, and with *that* particular method came from lots of different "slides" I had accumulated from lots of different sources. The same was true with personnel issues as well. The *why* is always more complex, yet it is the foundation for all we do. It was the clarion call to inspire them to get out of the limited thinking sometimes so familiar to the fire service culture.

It was a continuous process for me, too. I had to pour my thoughts through a strainer sorting out my own bias and prejudices in the process. I found when I have a clear, or clearer, picture of what is expected or desired, I operate from a much better perspective. My decision-making improves and my ability to formulate answers based on projections became clearer. The slides I add are from a much sturdier platform. Granted, experience adds greatly to this, but it also took a commitment from me personally to go out and discover this information instead of merely *waiting* for it to appear. It really boiled down to me having a desire for change and improvement; something that didn't just come from a book, it came from the heart. That additional knowledge gave me the confidence to put myself out there and keep putting one foot in front of the other.

It takes a lot of work to keep learning, expanding, and staying inspired. However, that growth is critical to staying ahead of the crowd and keeping life from being a coasting experience. It would have been easy for me to stay in the fire department "box." Trust me, over time I had the system down and knew what was "expected" of me. It's just

I'm not a "box" type of girl. Plus, life is much more interesting on the cutting edge. I couldn't let my fears hold me back. I had to bust out of my limited thinking and be a slide all unto myself.

No one will question your integrity if your integrity is not questionable.

~Nathaniel Bronner, Jr.
pastor & scientist

I have mentioned integrity several times, and most likely will talk about it again because it's so important. Integrity can mean different things to different people. For me, integrity means owning my actions in and throughout my entire life. What that means is that I own up to and take responsibility for my actions, right or wrong. If I do something that hurts another, I need to take responsibility for my actions and make it right. If I choose to do nothing, I take responsibility for that, too. Either way I don't blame, shift, or ignore my role in it; I stand tall and take whatever heat comes my way. Essentially, my word becomes my behavior. If my word fails to mimic my behavior I will not be seen as credible or reliable. I can't fight for diversity and not take a stand on it, too. I have to walk my talk as much, if not more, than others to be heard and taken seriously.

You may have heard the saying, "integrity is what you do when no one is watching." Even if someone is watching, there are some things to think about, like: Do you gossip about others, and then when they enter the room, act nice to them? Do you tell off-color jokes and then get offended when someone else tells one? Or, do you use sexual innuendoes and then get mad at a member of the opposite sex if they come on to you? Never forget, people are watching us, and *we* teach them how to treat us. If our integrity is in place and we are practicing what we preach, our lives go much smoother. When I am coaching people, I listen to what they say is going on in their lives, as this provides clues about where they are out of integrity or heading in that direction. It doesn't take long for me to see where they are living a double standard. We can't expect people to treat us with integrity when we are out of integrity ourselves.

Integrity is a foundation for all relationships, from our relationship with ourselves to our relationships with others: it intertwines our entire life. This is as true for work relationships as it is for our personal ones. Patterns get set-up, expectations made, and feelings get involved. It's important to understand we teach each other how we like to be treated by our own actions and responses. People don't always know how to behave or act around us. They receive those cues from what we project. It is so important to pay attention to how we are feeling, and make sure we are setting ourselves up for positive relationships and environments. One way to set ourselves up for success is to be clear on our priorities. They should line up like this:

Integrity 1st
Needs 2nd
Wants 3rd

We should never compromise our integrity for something we want. I can say from experience when I have denied my integrity for a need or want, I have regretted it. I learned this lesson early . . . in second grade. One thing, which was really fun about that year, was we were able to bring in items to present to the class. When we brought a toy, we sat it on a certain cabinet until time to share. Since the items we brought were up on top of the cabinet, we were able to view and admire them all day long. Some kids brought in some really awesome toys, and one toy I fell in love with was a small metal airplane. As we were getting our packs ready to go home, I stole the plane and hid it in my backpack. I really wanted it; it looked like so much fun. That night I played with it in secret, as I knew it was wrong to take it, and when I was finished playing, I hid it so my parents wouldn't see it. The next day in school I overheard the teacher and the student whose airplane I had taken, talking. The boy was sobbing and the teacher was trying to comfort him. In that moment, an overwhelming sense of embarrassment and guilt came over me and I regretted my decision greatly. That night when I got home, the plane that had fascinated and intrigued me now felt like a hot poker of shame. I took the plane with me to school the next day and when no one was looking, I returned it to the shelf. To this day, I remember the humiliation, disgrace, and discomfiture of what I did. It changed how I did things. I could no longer pretend my actions didn't affect others. Nor could I ignore the feeling of shame in gaining something by fraudulent purposes. That metal airplane changed my priorities.

Just like being "crazy" is a choice, so is living in integrity. I like to think of it as living my life as if it would show up on the front page of the newspaper. Would I be embarrassed, ashamed, or proud of what was reported about me? That plane story would not have made me proud. I have used this concept when I feel torn in making a decision. What would either choice look like on the front page? Am I doing it because it is right or just easy? Integrity doesn't always mean the easy way. In fact, it can be down right hard at times, but my experience is that things always end better when I stay in integrity than just do whatever is easiest. Another benefit of staying in integrity is that I have less agonizing choices to make; my life seems to run more smoothly. I don't like feeling that hot poker of shame.

When I took on the Fire Department with my lawsuit, I knew I might have to go to trial about it at some time. Because of this, I knew I had to keep my story in integrity. I couldn't change things to make me look better or embellish elements to make my case stronger. I had to tell the truth, the whole truth, and nothing but the truth. To do that I had to stay in integrity with my story, I couldn't morph it to make it sound better to one person versus the next. I believe I kept my story intact and in integrity for the entire 12 years before the case was settled. I'm glad I was able to do it, as staying in integrity made it possible to talk about the situation with others and still feel good about myself. I didn't compromise my integrity over my needs and wants for the outcome of the case. If the case had gone to trial, I would have been a good witness. I would have sworn to tell the truth, the whole truth, and I would have pulled it off. Integrity is the only way to go, if simply because it makes your life work better and feel better.

Integrity can sometimes be a tricky and elusive thing though. How I viewed the interactions and events in my life made it hard to determine when I was acting outside of integrity. In fact, sometimes it felt like integrity only to find out later, filled with regret, my ego has pulled a fast one on me. Ego is very powerful, and it had a very vested interest in keeping me like I was. It thought it was "protecting" me when in reality, it was doing just the opposite by keeping me locked in a belief system that is outdated, no longer serving me, and frankly, downright destructive. Why did I so often succumb to the will of my own ego? Because, it's like an old friend. There is a saying, "It's better to dance with the devil you know than the one you don't." The ego's ideas can be the same. Some of the ego's strategies are developed when we are in some crises, probably childhood, as survival mechanisms to help us endure in a very complicated world. At a young age, those reactions may have been wonderful and kept us safe. In adulthood, though, it keeps us from getting promoted, having meaningful relationships, and may cause us to end up being very lonely. The "computer program" we developed back then to survive is now a malignant virus that has its tentacles out choking off important aspects of our lives.

Therapists refer to these "viruses" or reoccurrences of patterns as *déjà-vu's*. They can lay dormant in our lives and then something happens, usually a trauma, and bang, we suddenly are no longer ourselves, but instead we are operating in fear and confusion, unable to focus, losing sleep. Life, suddenly, isn't working like it was before. Most likely, just like when we open a virus email, the dormant emotion from the past, and all the emotions associated with it, are brought up front and center and we get slapped to the floor. I experienced that with my emails from work. It has taken me many years and lots of work to figure out my déjà-vu reaction.

I got a clue that I was in a déjà-vu when I was at a woman's retreat and the woman running it turned to me and said bluntly that I didn't take any risks. I was pissed! *Of course I take risks*, I thought. *My god, didn't I sue my department? That was a risk!* She said, "Sure, that was a risk, but that was also the last one you have taken in a long time." I left that weekend very confused. Did I quit taking risks? Did I quit living life, quit stretching myself, and stop being in the flow of living? When I honestly examined it, I discovered I really had stopped taking risks. What I found was I kept hitting a core issue for me, which was the belief that *I didn't matter.* It's no wonder with that core issue that I kept hitting it within the fire department! It was an open wound that just never seemed to heal. As I reflect now, I see how this issue permeated my whole life, showing up many times in different scenarios. It was very frustrating, too, I knew I was sitting on some emotion, some trigger, but I couldn't see it. I would get caught up in the drama, blaming it on those around me, running away—hence not taking risks in order to avoid that "feeling" I couldn't identify.

When I was in the midst of my fire department career, I didn't have perspective enough to really *see* this block. In fact, it's only been recently that I've been in a safe enough space to see how my feelings of, "I don't matter," were running in the background, unconsciously affecting all my choices and interactions. It was through a series of personal blows in rapid succession, and a true desire to work through my emotional turmoil, that I was finally able to see this emotional limitation. As a result of letting it go, I am realizing *I DO matter.* I had to start letting go of some unhealthy attachments and now, I feel like I have been released from my emotional shackles. Will I hit this core issue again? Probably. But from now on, I will move through it much more quickly because I have an awareness of it. Now, I get to be my own champion and cheerleader, encouraging myself through every challenge. I couldn't have done this without real courage–to look into the depths of my soul and have the willingness to explore that part of me, which I was afraid to look at or shine a light on.

It was my ego that kept me sane but stuck in *I don't matter*. According to my ego, I was just fine. I needed to keep a low profile, adapt, and modify, do what was expected and things would be okay. However, I knew the things I learned at a young age that got me through successfully, as I aged, were like a noose around my neck, slowly squeezing the life out of me, one breath at a time. I was coasting, albeit on a slow decline; it was there and I could feel it. I needed to change and start living life, start growing and taking risks, emotionally and mentally. Sure, I studied for the captain's and battalion chief's tests and passed, but intellect was not my stretch, feeling with my emotions was my stretch–vulnerability and intimacy–now those two words would bring me to my knees.

I went on to do many more retreats with this woman whom I grew to both love and hate, sometimes all in the same moment. I spent a lot of time shaken to my core, learning about intimacy and how to connect with my emotions and learning what it meant to be truly vulnerable; it still scares me. She pushed every button I knew I had and more that I didn't even know, or want to know, that I had. I explored intimacy (or in-to-me-see) and vulnerability to the point that I can now set healthy boundaries with others without feeling like I have to lose myself in the process. As I moved through these feelings, I was able to uncover the emotions holding me back and keeping me hostage. It also gave me a toolbox that helped me navigate life's ups and downs and that, thankfully, pushed me to see where I was holding myself back. Now that "I matter," I love *me* a lot more and I'm less afraid to take risks. I also embrace integrity as a way of life. My life is starting to work . . . again.

Integrity is more than being honest with others. Some of the hardest work I had to do was being honest with myself–telling myself the truth–no more lies, no more coloring it up to look nicer, no more trying to make it smell better. What was always amazing was when I faced those fears head on and walked into them, they dissolved. I also discovered I wasn't alone. After years of working with groups of people and doing breakthrough work, I have found we are all closely linked, our fears so alike. When I started sharing, I found out I'm not so screwed up and we can, "let it go." Integrity is simply being real–being totally me. Do the actions I take fill me up or do they bring me down mentally, emotionally, or spiritually? If I don't like the answer, then I need to begin doing things daily which fill me up in those areas. I don't let the child in me run the adult me. I honor my inner child, thank it for its assistance in getting me through what I needed to get through, and then I let it go with love and gratitude. I tell my ego thanks but I've got things covered now, because you know what? I do! I got back in the driver's seat of life and on track. My life's back and I'm following the road signs to the real and authentic me. Living in integrity is what put me in the carpool lane of life, passing a lot of stuck traffic–and that feels really good.

SECTION 3

What to do when it's over . . .

Move on. *It is just a chapter in the past, but don't close the book–just turn the page.*

~Unknown

CHAPTER 16

The choir of heavenly angels

Music expresses that which cannot be put into words and cannot remain silent.

~*Victor Hugo*
French poet & activist

I was about eight years into fighting my case, getting my nails done with the same gal I had been seeing since the case had started, when she said something that really struck me. This woman had heard most of my rants about the case and had been a sympathetic ear throughout my ordeal. We had gone through a stretch where I was hoping it would either be settled or move forward and I was telling her about my frustrations with the case when she asked, "What are you waiting for, a choir of heavenly angels to start singing, signifying it's over?" To which I responded, "They aren't?" Well, I hate to burst your bubble but I found out a host of heavenly angels will not break out in heavenly tunes when it settles!

Her question was very poignant, though. When my case did finally settle, I found out, not only was there no host of singing angels; there was a whole other level of healing I had to go through.

One thing, which surprised me, (other than the angels not singing) was that when the case was settled, I was left with a void in my life. Things were too quiet. I used to describe the case to others as similar to TV static. For those of you who aren't old enough to remember, at midnight the TV stations would quit broadcasting and you would see a gray screen and hear static. It was like a constant gravelly buzz—that was what my lawsuit was like. It was like that buzz—a sound that was easy to forget about but with only a thought, it would be noticeable again. It was never completely out of my thoughts; it just wasn't front-and-center all the time. When I had to do things involved with the case, it was very noticeable and "loud" and then the noise would fade to the background as things died down, back to its almost unnoticeable "hum," but never gone. When it was finally settled, the sound turned off but not the memory of it. That buzz was strangely missed.

It was like I needed to have something to do to fill the void left behind. I had been on a crusade for the last 12 years, and now, it was . . . over. It was very un-dramatic, too. I went to my lawyer's office, signed some papers, we took some pictures, I got some flowers and then I took my copies home with me. I sat in my car after I left the lawyer's office, feeling numb. I pulled away from the curb and got about a block away before I burst into tears. They weren't happy tears either; they were more like surviving something tears. As I drove away crying, I was thinking, *I survived, I made it through, I made it . . .* I *had* indeed survived.

For the next couple of days, I was in a space where I felt like I needed to pinch myself to be sure I was awake and it was really over. I made the calls to family and friends and shared the good news, I had won and it was over. I was happy it was over, mind you, I really was. But underlying it was also the realization that I was a survivor, too. And I was pissed . . .

When I filed my lawsuit in 1996, I took my lawyers advice and I did become the "best lil' firefighter I could be" and put my emotions on the back burner. At the time, it was too much for me to feel, and later, it wouldn't have been good for the case for me to be emotional. So, for 12-years, I "pretended" the lawsuit didn't hurt. I kept up that illusion for a long time, and it kept me sane and able to put one foot in front of the other. I had no idea of the tsunami of emotions that would come to the surface all over again after it was settled. In spite of all the work I had done on myself, an emotional tidal wave came crashing in.

In the months that followed, I came about the closest I ever came to being disciplined for insubordination. I was so pissed that it didn't take much for management to push my buttons. I became obstinate and mouthy. I was walking around saying I had 500,000 reasons to be pissed, and did they want to hear reason 347,452? Not a good thing when you were a battalion chief and expected to keep the troops under your command in line.

We settled the case for $500,000, and I had almost as many hurts to express.

Shortly after winning, I remember sitting in the administrative officer's office talking about various things when he brought up diversity. That day he said enough trigger words to send me into a tailspin that had me spitting words out of my mouth. Luckily for me, another battalion chief and friend was in the office with me and she literally grabbed my arm and pulled me out. Although she agreed with what I had been saying, my lack of decorum, professionalism, and objectivity was not in place to be having the impact it needed to change anyone's opinion, let alone someone that needed coaching and leadership to show him how to model it. I was simply delivering a couple dozen of the 500,000 justifiable reasons for being upset. The problem was, he was simply a pawn in the system that was still in transition and I was in no emotional state to be an advocate in that moment. Thank goodness I had a friend that pulled the pit-bull that was me off the guy! It was shortly after, I realized a change had occurred, and the beginning of the end of my fire service career had begun.

What about the money? Everyone was curious about it. Well, let me tell you the number is way more impressive than the actual dollars and cents. Four hundred thousand dollars went to my team of three lawyers. I was lucky my main lawyer was smart and knew that the judgment was taxable and had the county write two checks, one to her and one to me so I wouldn't have to pay taxes on theirs as well as mine. That's right–taxes, Title 7 judgments are taxable. Out of mine, I paid the 30% to taxes, about $20,000 in expenses, and the rest went to bills and a vacation.

At the beginning, I had grand plans to put some of it into savings but the funny part was . . . it felt like blood money, and, when it came down to it, I didn't want to have any of it sitting around. I know that sounds strange, but it was true. It didn't feel like something I wanted to have around me. I wanted it all gone. I never did this for the money in the first place. In a lot of ways, it would never be enough in my heart to "pay" for my emotional toll–there was no amount that would ever cover that. The money felt dirty to me. I'm glad I was able to pay off my bills and our vacation was a lot of fun with many fond memories, but the greatest part is the fact I won, not the dollars I aquired. One thing I know for sure, if you file a lawsuit for the money, you are doing it for all the wrong reasons.

You have to prepare yourself for a lot of out-comes when going through these things. I'd forgot-ten how many times we were "going to trial" only to back down as they went back to the table. From my lawyer's standpoint, it was business as usual. From mine, it was nerve racking, hence the emotional rollercoaster. While it was good to get off that rollercoaster, it was like I felt after an amusement park action ride; I felt like I was on unsteady ground for a while, until I found my equilibrium again.

As a firefighter, I was naturally addicted to adrenaline, and although the case took 12 years, there was still some adrenaline attached to it. My husband and I had many conversations about the *end* and what impact it would have on me and on us as a couple. I know now, no amount of talking truly prepared me. I really was surprised to realize how angry I still was. I was under the delusion that I could "think" away the pain. I've come to understand I can talk about my pain, I can write about my pain, but I can only let it go by feeling it. I've been told we can release any pain or tragedy (such as a death in the family) from our emotions in three minutes, if we totally feel it, down to our toes. I'm not sure I've met anyone capable of doing that. I do know I now allow myself the space to feel grief. I realize now how important it is in life to feel my feelings. I also realize how it creates stress when I don't.

Grief is more prevalent than we realize. We all recognize the loss of a parent as grief but the loss of a boyfriend/girlfriend? Job? Discrimination? Someone mean to us at the coffee house for no reason? A bad day? Anytime I have a loss, however small, I experience a form of grief and I should honor it as such and grieve. Maybe it's a good cry or talking to a friend or a therapist. The point is

I can't hold on to it. All emotions need to be in flow, in then out, like breathing, grief and grieving, too. Will I always "get over it" in one day? Maybe or maybe not, but if I don't keep letting it flow, it gets stuck. I saw so many patients over the years, as we went on calls, who were stuck in the past–so stuck they were dying of it. It amazed me how many angry people we came across on calls, too. They weren't happy people, and you could see it in their eye–under the anger and rage–scared, lonely, abandoned, feeling like wounded animals and lashing out at anyone who might dare to help. What they really wanted was love, a hug, comfort but they had become porcupines with quills so sharp, no one could get close enough to give them what they desired. Their emotions had backed up, the stress etched on their faces, disease ravaging their bodies, to the point they didn't even know which way to turn for help, or how to accept it if it came. It was sad.

I'm aware how that could have been me. I was very blessed to have had great people in my life who pushed me when I was incapable of pushing myself. I am also lucky I was brave enough and strong enough to ask myself the tough questions that got my ego to move aside to allow some healing to begin. I had to feel that grief down to my toes, and yes, it took way more than three minutes. Even a couple of years after settling the lawsuit, I still occasionally get a pang or two, and I still occasionally see a therapist to help erase the effects of that déjà vu. I can say, in all honesty, that I'm starting to hear a flute and a couple of horns of angelic caliber in the background, and it sure sounds sweet! It may not be a choir of heavenly angels but the music I'm making is the beat from my new drum and band. I kind of like it . . .

SECTION 4

Do you really have what it takes?

Strength does not come from physical capacity. It comes from an indomitable will.

~Mahatma Gandhi
spiritual & political leader

Consider how hard it is to change yourself and you'll understand what little chance you have in trying to change others.

~Benjamin Franklin
statesman & philosopher

Over the years, I have had many men and women come up to me and ask for my advice about some situation they were facing. You might think I would be pro-lawsuit, but actually, nine times out of ten, I advised them to think of other solutions. Most of the time, it was more about their feelings and not about real violations. It was always hard to listen to their stories; there was a part of me that wanted to run into their boss' office (or co-worker's) and chew them out for the treatment they were giving that person. Over time, I tempered that urge as I moved up in rank and realized these situations were more multi-faceted than at first glance. One of the best examples of this was a story someone told me early in my career. It was a story about a rabid dog.

I was experiencing a crisis with another person in the department when my friend told me this story. The details aren't important, just the story which illustrated the behavior of others when details are unclear. He told me about a dog, a normal dog that had been playing, and as a result, its salvia had foamed. He said those looking on with the idea that the dog had rabies would see a rabid dog, when in fact, all that was wrong with the dog is it had been playing hard and needed a drink of water. It was all about perception. If you were looking for a dog with rabies, I can easily see how you might misinterpret the situation. However, with some investigation, you would probably figure out the dog's actions didn't jive with the symptoms you were seeing which would make you step back and re-evaluate. I found this story to be true with people, too. When we have a mindset that discrimination (as an example) is going on, we tend to see it all around us. I use a radar screen as another example. When you start researching a car or truck that you want to buy, you start seeing others like it all over town? Now, if you think about it, I'm sure you will agree the vehicle was not suddenly showing up to a greater degree, but your perception and/or notice of it is heightened. When this happens, it simply shows up on your mental radar screen making it more visible to you. The same is true with discrimination, violence, any bad thing you fear or are hypersensitive to; the same can be true of good stuff. You start seeing the rabid dog, or rainbows (for that matter), all over the place. Remember, perception is a choice and that is why it is so important to discriminate between hurt feelings and real violations. Both can have the same effect but you need to be clear in your perception to differentiate between the two.

After I mentally filed my rabid dog theory and listened to their stories, I couldn't help but think how they had some responsibility in what was going on with their situations. Just as I believe some of my own actions had contributed to my problems, I had to really listen to what their whole story was before I sent them off to a potentially long, arduous legal battle. Did they really have a case or were they simply experiencing hurt feelings? One quote I love is from The One Minute Manager by Kenneth Blanchard, Ph.D. and Spencer Johnson, M.D.:

If you can't tell me what you'd like to be happening, you don't have a problem yet. You're just complaining. A problem only exists if there is a difference between what is actually happening and what you desire to be happening. Said another way . . . I do not want to hear about only attitudes or feelings. Tell me what is happening in observable, measurable terms.

It is this type of thinking that separates hurt feelings from real violations. When you take your "case" to your employer and/or court of law, they don't want to hear about your feelings on the matter. They want to hear *just the facts*. If all you can offer up is, "It hurt my feelings," you are likely to have a problem and the argument will turn into a he said/she said situation where perceptions get in the way. To have a strong legal argument, you need to show it violates the law—your feelings are just a by-product. Also, remember, you can't maintain hurt feelings for 12 years! You have to have something more substantial to hang onto. Were my feelings hurt by what happened? Absolutely! However, in the 12 years it took to fight this, I also grew a lot professionally and personally. To survive, I had to adapt and grow. If all I had was those hurt feelings to maintain my battle, I would be hard pressed to think of where I would be now. My guess is I would have been a bitter person. No one can make you feel anything–you choose how you feel. I was able to keep this from being a "personal battle of wills" to a legal battle by not reacting to my hurt feelings. This is no easy feat; it took a lot of moxie to not respond to my rabid dog and not see everything that involved a hint of discrimination on my radar screen. It was a learned behavior but one that was easier because I had a strong legal argument behind me.

How do you know if you are reacting to hurt feelings or real violations? Real violations are measurable and observable. Not only are they offensive, *they are against the law.* They will stand up in a trial. I'm not saying hurt feelings aren't real; they are very real. The hardest part about fighting discrimination is it rarely reaches the legal realm and stays mainly at that lower level of hurt feelings, which is what makes it so difficult to defend against. It is death by a thousand cuts, and although a couple of cuts may not hurt much at first, as they mount up, they do eventually hurt, and hurt a lot. What is so hard to get others to understand is this is not *only* about the victim; *it hurts the organization just as much.*

When I first became captain, things were tough, really tough. I was set up for failure by individuals who were very well respected, and others just followed their lead. I was walking a tightrope over whether to say anything or just hang on and ride it out. Most of the time, I just held on. There was way more of them than me and I needed to keep my sanity (or what little I had left) intact. I had a discussion with my crew when I became captain. I told them I was under a microscope and by default so were they. I told them they would be asked about how it was to work with me and what it was like at our station. Although I couldn't tell them what to say, I did want to caution them and let them know that indirectly they would be affected by the stories that got out. If we had solidarity, respected each other, and related little to those who inquired looking for dirt on me, they would eventually tire of digging, things would die down and everything would be okay. If they chose to get in the fray, it would affect *all* of us negatively, and we would *all* pay. The decision was truly theirs.

Luckily for me, they chose solidarity and even came back and told me how surprised they were at the dirt others wanted on me. Not only did they have my back, they also started having fun with it and made me appear even bigger than life at times. Of course, no one believed them, but it stopped the rumormongers and we were able to get back to being a normal crew. Eventually, it was no fun to dig for dirt about me because my crew was tight. I'd spent a lot of time bonding with them as individuals and I appreciated them. I looked for special talents they had and capitalized on them, frequently asking for their insights and inspirations of how to handle situations we had. It always amazed me when they would tell me I was one of few captains they had worked with who trusted them like that. In my mind, I was simply holding them as capable and they were simply rising to the occasion.

People are really funny. I once was on a call in a "bad" side of town where I carried a hefty four D-cell battery flashlight because it might be necessary to protect my crew and myself. We went into a home and were met by a 6'4", very large (and I mean ice box sized) man standing there, very threatening, blocking our way to the patient. I was leading the way so I was standing in front of him with my flashlight and clipboard, all 5'5" of me, not a threat at all. He growled down at me and asked, *"Are you goin' use that flashlight on me?"* and I bellowed up at him, *"Am I going to have to?"* At the same time, both of us realized how ridiculous it was to even think I could actually do that and in an instant, we both started laughing. He moved aside and let us do what we needed to do. It was clear to me early on that I had to come up with another way to deal with men. Let's face it, I wasn't going to win in a fistfight, even with a four D-cell flashlight!

One of my male friends in the department would often jokingly say to me, "You know, I can beat you up," and I would banter back, "But I know you won't!" We'd both laugh but I think by acknowledging, you-can-beat-me-up-but-that's-not-the-best-way-to-handle-this, helped me open the door to better communication. There might have been a couple of firefighters on the department I could have taken in a fistfight but the majority would have taken me down quickly. It didn't take rocket scientist skills to know I needed to come up with a better way to get these men to listen to me. I'm glad I had to rely on my brains more than brawn in developing my management skills. In the long run, I was the winner because of it.

I wouldn't recommend brawn even if you were as big as an icebox. People don't work at their best when they are working from fear. I had to make sure to develop conversation and communication skills and practice them daily. The best course, as a supervisor, was to find a strategy that worked at integrating me with them. I had to balance it with a life outside of my job so my ego was not dependent on their opinion of me. It kept me more objective and stable. I had to maintain my integrity and display the very attitudes and behaviors I wanted to receive from others. That helped a lot. If I found there was a violation of the law, I documented it, took pictures, and said, "NO!"

in clear and definitive terms. I had to be clear on what I expected but also willing to work on solutions. If I found someone acting in an inappropriate manner, I let him or her know up front. I tried not to let bad behavior go on for any length of time. This can be difficult if you are new, but it's not smart to wait until you finally get to the end of your rope either. Remember, in some ways you have been "training" them by not setting boundaries, so try not to vomit it out all at once, give them time to adapt, too. If a real violation occurs, handle it immediately and deal with it professionally with the intention they want it corrected as much as you do and it's as good for them as it is for you. Stay in integrity. Don't embellish on the circumstances to make a story better, but by the same token, don't back down to spare feelings. If it's happening to you, most likely it's happening to others, and, it needs to be dealt with immediately. Seek support. Seek legal advice. Stay centered and re-read this book! You'll be okay.

Let the justice system or grievance process figure it out, if you aren't sure. Quit being a silent victim. You are worth being heard. One day, you will figure out why you are in the situation. There is always a silver lining to be found in the end. Hang on and really look at how you can make a difference where you are. You are there for a reason and *you* matter.

It's one thing to feel that you are on the right path, but it's another to think that yours is the only path.

~Paulo Coelho
Brazilian lyricist & novelist

Filing any lawsuit is not a process for the weak of heart. In fact, I like to describe it as being akin to pregnancy. There's no such thing as "kind of pregnant." You are either all in or all out, there is no in between. The same goes for lawsuits. The average wait time from filing to resolution for Title 7 discrimination cases is three to seven years. Some may be settled sooner, but some may be much longer, as in my case.

One of the saddest thoughts I had when I put the whole process in perspective was how it related to my family. When I started this process, my oldest son was in kindergarten and when the case was settled, he was graduating from high school. It saddens me greatly that through most of my sons' lives neither knew their mother without this legal issue hanging over her head, and they felt the stress and strain, which cropped up throughout the years. I can tell you without a doubt that if this case had only been about hurt feelings, I would never have had the resolve to see it to the end. I felt this was bigger than I was and, therefore, important enough for me to pursue, regardless of the personal tolls.

There were many times I wanted to quit. There were many times when my marriage reached its breaking point, even after the case was settled. If I had not been committed to the higher ideal, I would never have lasted. I knew this was a battle that the women in our department needed to win. Regardless of who handled the battle, it had to be done, one way or another; it was too important. It turned out that responsibility fell to me. I could have easily moved back into the dorm room, put my head into the sand—gone along to get along— and I probably would have avoided the whole email retribution. But I didn't. I chose to draw my line, to say, "No more!," and fight. I never wavered from my belief that this was important to not only me, but to all the women, and consequently the men, in our department, too. That is what got me through the "down days," the days I would have loved to have just been Mommy, unburdened by the case. Apparently, it wasn't in my life plan.

Many have asked me over the years, "Would you do it all over again?" The answer has always been a resounding, "Yes!" The issue I filed about was bigger than I was, and I felt a very personal responsibility to see it through. What happened to me, and many of the other women in our department, needed to be changed. Like I said before, mine was not the worst that some women suffered. I had the legal recourse and the incentive to pursue it. My case was built around systemic discrimination in which I claimed my mistreatment was not only happening to me but also all of the other women in our department. I always took that very seriously and whenever I heard a story from another fire-fighter, it only reinforced my commitment to see this to the end. This was a crusade for me, and for all of the women in my department.

I look back now and sometimes wonder if there was any arrogance in that feeling of being a *crusader*. I mean, it's not like any of the other women on the department came up to me and said, "Gina, will you take this one on for us?" I simply assumed they wanted it as much as I did. Sadly, that wasn't always the case.

You have to be careful with assumptions. I have heard it said as "making an ass-out-of-you-and-me," meaning that in the end, you both look bad when assumptions are made. I'm not saying the women wanted discrimination in our department. What I'm saying is there were as many opinions on the cause of the issues, and solutions for it, as there were firefighters–women included. There were also a fair number who thought my vocal stance on discrimination was the source of many of their indirect problems, which I can't say is true or not true. Again, perception is a choice, and making assumptions can get you in trouble. Either way, it can be perceived as arrogant to think I was *crusading* for the women of our department. I have no doubt they thought they could take care of themselves–thank you very much!

This was, in my own small way, my Frederick Douglass moment. I had to look at myself and determine what rights I had as a person and a firefighter. I could no longer submit to the injustice imposed upon me, and I had to do something. In that instant, I had to believe in myself, take advantage of the situation, and use my power of language to affect a positive change. A door opened that day at the station, when they wanted to move me illegally; I saw the door, recognized the opportunity, and stepped through it. I had a vision of the workplace without discrimination and I wanted it. I wanted it bad. It was on my radar screen, as I was already becoming an advocate. When the stars lined up, I simply reacted, moved forward, and took a stand. Maybe there was some arrogance on my part, I really did (and do) feel I was making a difference for all women firefighters that day. That was what gave me the resolve and fortitude to stay the course and remain afloat in the dark of night in a very stormy sea. Was the sentiment misplaced? Maybe a little, I never asked them for their input, I just did it. Was it ever *not* from the heart? No! It was completely from my heart and I was totally committed to seeing it through, even if it never was for anyone other than me.

How do you decide to pursue legal action? First, you think long and hard about it. It's not something to take lightly or go into without a strong foundation in not only legal support, but also personal support. Get good advice; then search your heart. This is not something you can take on and then turn away from. It's a commitment, and it's one that has some very real consequences for you and your family. Initiating a lawsuit is not something you can cry wolf about, because if you do, you will not only lose credibility, but also some self-respect. If you are convinced there are some real violations then I feel you have an obligation to do something. I never understood those who saw it happening, or had it happen to them, who stood by and said nothing. I am more lenient now and much more understanding of those who choose to back down. It's hard work to be under a microscope during a legal action, but on the other hand, I often wonder how could they just let it go? In those "moments," one truly gets to see their character and have a chance for true-life changes. Remember, we don't exist in a vacuum and our actions viewed by others may serve as the catalyst for remarkable transformation and change. One person *does* make a difference.

As that favorite saying that's so adequately appropriate goes, "Evil does flourish when good men (and women) do nothing." It always amazes me to watch or hear about some horrendous act against a woman, watch her start to fight it, see the situation die down enough that the heat's off of her, and see her drop it only to be back in the fray two to six months later. I can sympathize with wanting to let it go when the pressure is off, but it's a bit delusional to think it won't happen again.

Do you know how you build trust? It's done through consistent behavior displayed over time. If six months later you are back in the trenches with them all over again on *any* matter, you can pretty much trust it will continue until it is dealt with thoroughly. Sometimes, as women, we think we should be "nice" and make sure everyone is having a good time, enjoying himself or herself. Completing grievance and discipline paperwork on your co-workers or bosses probably won't fall under any of those "should's" we've been brought up with, so when they start playing our game of being nice again, we think we are back on high ground and the *heat* isn't needed anymore. If only it were that simple.

In reality, what we've done is train them to do a magic trick, which may look good on the surface, as sleight of hand usually does, but in reality, it's just that, a trick. And guess what, *we are the losers in this game.* It's been sad to see some of the women in my department play this game with the powers that be. Eventually what happens is the woman isn't seen as serious; she's ignored, talked about horribly behind her back and held with very little respect. On her side, I see her develop a mountain of bitterness because her sense of right/wrong gets so out of whack from denying it for so long she ends up spewing it from her pores. I'm being a little dramatic, but look at the faces of people like this in your organization—they are the ones who are old before their years—they're the deer in the headlights, everyone-is-out-to-get-me type of people. Those at higher levels in my department may have hated me for a while in the beginning, but, in the end, they knew I had a line and they didn't dare cross it without knowing they would have to answer for it. They knew my bark was followed by a solid bite and while they may not have liked me much, they did respect me, if only because they knew where I stood.

It's a tough decision–do I stand and fight or do I back down? Either choice can be right or wrong. That's why you really need to talk it over with people you trust and who support you by giving honest feedback. You have to see the big picture. Can I, in good conscience, walk away, leaving this for others to have to deal with and clean up? Am I just walking away because I got what I wanted for right now and not what's right? These are good questions. Take time to consider the answers. For a while, you might not be a "good" firefighter or employee by the definition of those around you. But let me tell you, good comes and goes, but *respect* stays. If you have a choice between being accepted or respected, always pick respected. It will take you much further and pay you back with much more confidence in yourself and in others. Whatever your decision, to pursue or back down, make sure it is on your terms and for the right reasons. Every night, the last image you see in the mirror is your own. That is the person to whom you need to be the truest and the one you have to ultimately respect. Be committed to *you*.

I try to take one day at a time, but sometimes
several days attack me at once.

~*Jennifer Yane*
artist & writer

One thing I wished someone had told me would
happen when I filed a lawsuit was that all my
personal issues would come up, and not only those
around the legal aspect of the case. I realized I
didn't live in only the fire department/case bubble. The case permeated my whole life, personal
and professional. I spent hundreds of hours on a
therapist couch and in seminars to work on releasing the inner demons this case brought up, and in
some ways, still does.

During this process, I realized I was laying my
issues with my job and my case on other people
in my life. The angry boss got projected onto my
husband when I felt he wasn't being fair. My father
became the unreasonable co-worker, my mom the
misunderstood Gina. It was confusing at times and
very frustrating. You recall the beach conversation

with my parents and them suggesting I sue? A few years into the lawsuit, I went to my mom to ask her if she would be willing to help support me financially by fronting the money for depositions and some legal fees, because it looked like the case was moving to trial and I would be responsible for those fees out-of-pocket. My mom looked at me and said, "Well, will you win?" I was so hurt and devastated by her answer. I thought to myself, *If I didn't think I would win, I wouldn't have filed the lawsuit!* She may not have meant it the way it sounded but at the time, her response cut like a knife. It was then I made a decision that anyone who did not support me in the belief I would win the case was out of my loop of support. I rarely talked about the case to my parents again after that discussion.

I simply couldn't entertain the thought I wouldn't win. After so many years of my life invested in this "nightmare," I realized I couldn't fight everyone. I was too fragile. I was already struggling to come to some middle ground where my marriage wouldn't fall apart, where I could function fully within the department, and even more importantly, not have the stress of the case influence my children. So, if you weren't on board my bus, it was leaving without you. I could understand the fire department not supporting me, but my parents? It took a lot of work to let that one go. My point is this was not only about the case, the lawsuit involved everyone around me, and some people who I believed would support me sometimes disappointed me. That was my perception. However, they didn't necessarily mean it in the way I took it. I found myself feeling so raw that I didn't have the perspective to counteract their reactions effectively especially when it came from family and friends. That is why it was so important to get professional help. My advice to a parent reading this: If you have someone you love involved in this type of process, or any other painful situation, don't ask him or her if they think they will win. You are their *support,* so support them. My advice is to be open to hearing about the situation and be a sounding board, when asked. Remember, until you have walked in their shoes, you really can't make an honest assessment on the validity of their case or situation. Leave that to the lawyers and judges. You be a loving and supportive family member or friend.

As I became more involved in healing myself, I realized I had the symptoms of Post Traumatic Stress Disorder (PTSD). Before I initiated the lawsuit, I commented that it was a bogus syndrome and people needed to "get real." I have another take on that now. There have been times when I have been taken to my knees from PTSD; similar to the feelings I had when those emails hit me. It's not a pretty place and one I avoid at all costs when I can. So, PTSD? It's real!

One of the PTSD symptoms I had was hyper vigilance. I was talking with a therapist as I was learning I was exhibiting symptoms of PTSD and we discovered it was showing up when it came to vacations. She asked me what I would take with me if I were to go on a trip or vacation, and I started listing everything I could possibly need as well as things I probably wouldn't, but wanted to be "prepared for." You could have asked my husband and he would have told you that when we went on vacations, my over-packing was legendary! As we started to break down my list, it became apparent I had some fears buried in that thought process. I had a hard time *not* being vigilant; I wanted to be prepared for anything that might come up so I wouldn't be exposed and vulnerable. This showed up in other areas of my life as well. I avoided things related to the case and things I didn't want to do in my life. This started a process of always being stressed and "in a hurry." I was over-sensitive to anything I perceived as scary and unknown. I was very lucky this didn't have an adverse affect on my career; it showed up primarily in my family life. This is partly why I stopped taking risks. It was a roundabout survival technique that really wasn't very effective. However, once you get on this kind of ride, it can be hard to get off. The first time I was able to pack a carry-on for a five-day trip, I felt liberated! I also realized I had all that I needed and didn't have to compromise either. It's great that my brain can think of all I might need when I'm gone, but my mind now knows what's important and helps me prioritize. PTSD is like a short circuit in the brain making it think too much or get tripped up by a bad "program." Like a bad computer virus, it needs to be treated so the circuit can reset and order can be restored.

Would you get PTSD if you started a lawsuit? Maybe not, but don't rule it out completely. This is why it is so important to have support, including the support of your lawyer. One of the hard things in my process was realizing I was simply a witness in my own case when it came to my lawyer's perspective. I was lucky my lawyer was as much a teacher as she was my representative. I acquired an incredible amount of legal information and she was constantly instructing me as to what we were doing and where we were going. I couldn't imagine not having a good, trusting relationship with her and the other two lawyers who were involved. If you don't feel the *vibe* with your lawyer, shop around. You won't always agree with them, that's not what I'm getting at. In this regard, *support* became a two-way street between my lawyer and me; I needed her support and I needed to support her empirical fact-finding. It took me awhile to *get* that I was there to prepare her to represent me and I didn't have to understand everything she did. Only *she* needed to get it, and it was my job to support her in representing me the best way possible for her. Make sure your lawyer understands you and respects you enough to be patient at times, too. Remember, you need to shut-up and listen to his or her legal advice!

Stress is a big part of the process in a legal action. In fact, it will play a major role in the whole scenario. The best way to cope with it is to acknowledge it and develop a strategy to deal with it from the beginning. As I've said before, a lot of stress is unresolved grief. There is so much great literature about grief, primarily about death and dying. I encourage you to check it out, because even if you think it wasn't a death and no one is dying, you are still under its effects if you have experienced discrimination, loss, or a stressful event of any kind. Whenever you go through a tragic event, it creates grief. We recognize and support people in grief when there is a death or serious illness, but most don't get it when the tragedy is less obvious. We don't always appreciate that victims of discrimination have to go through the five stages of grief just as if there was a death. Those five stages are:

1. Denial
2. Anger
3. Bargaining
4. Depression
5. Acceptance

I have experienced each one of these and am still working on that fifth step. I know that what got me through these phases towards acceptance was hope. I knew I couldn't lose hope throughout this process. When my mom made that comment asking me if I would win my case, it affected my hope, the one thing to which I was clinging. The loss of it was something I couldn't fathom. It was the anchor that kept me from drifting afloat in the ocean of uncertainty through this whole process. This book is a reflection of my acceptance and also some closure for me; it is also my gift of support and hope to others. I am beginning to accept that

I can move on and feel good about what happened during the time of my lawsuit. This is the silver lining I talked about, coming through the grief to the other side to acceptance and having hope for the future. That which does not kill you does, indeed, make you much stronger. It was my faith and hope, which ultimately pulled me through.

At times, I still get hit unexpectedly with PTSD, like when I was at a retirement party for a co-worker about a year after my own retirement. As part of the décor, they had a continuous slide presentation his friends made which proclaimed the great moments throughout his illustrious career. As I stood there watching the slides and seeing all the happy faces and times, my PTSD began to hit, grief started to curl around me like an octopus tentacle, choking me tighter with each new image. I left suddenly to avoid the breakdown which was threatening to let loose. It really hit me like a cannon ball. The good news was that within hours I knew what had happened and why. The bad news was it was still showing up, *and* when I least expected it. At least that time, I was able to love myself quickly back to "normal." Those pictures were reminders of my isolation, loss, and profound grief. That feeling of living in a fish bowl, always looking out, wanting to desperately be a part of the group, found me again, and for a moment, I was lost in that pain. I find it is holding me back less and less as I let myself really grieve. When I cry, I let myself feel it all the way to my toes. Sometimes, I even feel like I am going to throw up, although nothing ever comes up except the stuck emotions, which need releasing. I may still need more than three minutes to "get over it," but I am getting a lot better. The PTSD doesn't rule my life now as I am more in control and I process through it quickly. I feel ready to move forward, embrace my "new" life as a retired battalion chief and author, and see what's next for me. I know in my heart I have what it takes for the long haul. It was worth the ride, including the twists, turns, and complete U-turns, at times.

Filing a suit is not a short-term venture. It is an all-consuming task, which is not for the weak at heart. Each of us has our own story to tell and each story has in it lessons for the person who is telling and the one who is hearing it. How we manage these events and stories in our lives teaches us how to manage the next ones we will experience as life moves forward. There will be other challenges in my life over the years, but I am more confident I will survive, and even thrive, as I face them. I know there is a silver lining and that gets me to that acceptance even quicker. Now, I have a fantastic toolbox and a strong support system, which buoys me through those rough times we all face in life. Once someone I was coaching asked me why no one called her when they were in crisis. She was young and I explained to her that people call those who have effectively weathered the storms in their lives. They use them as a support to lean on. I explained she would get those calls as she effectively moved through her grief and became a pillar and lighthouse for others to follow, her example will show others how it can be done.

The important thing is not to get stuck in grief but honor it and express it as you move through it. It's essential to realize grief exists, and it's okay to feel whatever you feel–denial, anger, bargaining, or depression. What's not okay is to spend your life in one of those states. You need to keep moving–keep healing. I still honor that part of me that experiences grief and continue to heal myself daily by making it okay to be vulnerable and to feel. I know I have what it takes right inside of me. It's taken a lot of work, a lot of fantastic teachers, and a lot of time and money, but all of it has been well worth it–I found me in the process as you will find you . . .

I don't want to get to the end of my life and find that I have lived just the length of it. I want to have lived the width of it as well.

~Diane Ackerman
author

I was lucky I didn't have to face the reality of not winning, but I can assure you I had some thoughts on the matter over the years. What I have come to realize is that it's not always winning that makes change happen.

One thing that happens when you file any complaint is they have to look at their practices, regardless of whether they feel they have been wrong or not. It is in that *looking* that realization become reality. They no longer have the luxury of keeping their heads in the sand; they have to at least justify their actions in a public manner. Even if you don't prevail, the bottom line is they had to look at it and that shed some light on the matter. It opens a doorway, and through that door, change follows.

It's like looking into a dark room. As the door slightly opens, light begins to spill into the room illuminating the contents; this light starts to reveal what once lay in the shadows. Contents, once hidden, become identifiable and open for examination. It is no longer such a dark and scary place. The room's contents can be explored and perceptions adjusted. I simply opened the door; many others have pushed it open even further. Those open doors allow the truth to enter and bloom. It wouldn't have taken my win to accomplish that. Most of what I wanted from the department had been accomplished over the 12-years I fought for it. For me, the winning only gave them the incentive to keep that door wide open and the light shining in, making it easier for those who followed. In my case, the light is now firmly anchored into a room called diversity.

Your filing and/or complaint will likely have the same effect in your workplace. A door will be opened and the light of truth will have an avenue to follow. I would love to tell you it will happen quickly, but as you can probably gather already, it is not a quick fix, so be prepared to wait and be patient. I remember one particular fight with the department about remodeling one of our older station's sleeping and bathroom facilities. This process had been going on for several years with many meetings, phone calls, and me generally being a pest to them until it was finally in the works to begin. About a month before they were to break ground, a woman captain was assigned to the same station on another shift, where I'd been for about two years, and I was complaining to her about my frustration over getting the bathroom work started. She took it upon herself to "make some calls" and informed me the next shift that she got it taken care of and they would be there the next week to begin. She looked at me like I was incompetent; I didn't waste my time explaining to her all the work (and the lawsuit) it took to begin that project. In her mind, she made one call and it was taken care of. There was a part of me which wanted to scream at her that she was delusional, that she didn't know all the effort I had put into that remodel—most of which I had done without any publicity—and her call was just timely, not noteworthy. Instead, I bit my tongue and told her, "Good job!" It broke my heart, because I'd worked so hard for this, and she got to "claim the glory." The truth is, it doesn't matter who made it happen. The bottom line is, it finally happened.

If you are looking to be the role model for change, you will most likely find yourself with tire treads up your back. Of course, if you think about it, as the one who called them on the carpet, it is unlikely they will name a station after you in thanks for pointing out they screwed up. The best you can hope for is to be a part of the committee to make sure the changes implemented are truly diverse. You may find that a "shining knight" comes in at the last minute to take the glory and proclaim victory, leaving you mucking out the stables once again. I was glad I wasn't in it for the name recognition because it never came. The closest I got to a "thank you" was $500,000 and a sad three line thank you letter required in the settlement agreement. Some would claim that was enough, and maybe it should have been, but it sure hurt like hell when the other newly arrived female captain was proclaiming to all at the station how she took on the big guys and with one call slew the dragon for change. It made me feel like the whiney bitch that complained all the time. I knew the truth, but at times, it would have felt good if others did, too.

Sometimes being a pioneer sucks, but it has also given me the most tremendous growth experiences I could have ever thought possible. I have been stretched to my breaking point and guess what? I didn't break! Neither will you. At the end you will look back, regardless of whether you win or not, and realize you have gained some very valuable skills–maturity, confidence, lots of wisdom, and more. If I had to choose between recognition for getting a bathroom and sleeping quarters at a station, or the growth I got along the way, I would choose the growth hands down. The fire department was just a stage of life for me. We all go through stages–we go to school, then we're off to careers and family, and eventually, we reach the stage called retire-ment. This is the stage I am in now, and I entered it with a far greater vision of my life and world that was only possible because of my experiences in my life thus far. If I had not taken on the challenge of the lawsuit I would have cheated myself out of some of the most valuable lessons I could have ever learned about my world *and* myself. I weathered the storm and I am much stronger for the experience. I say to others, "Nothing scares me now, I've worked for the fire department!" That is probably an overstatement–I still get scared sometimes, but now, I know I will survive.

You might not win in a court of law, but I think any time you bring an issue into the light of day, it gets examined. You've all seen the Discovery Channel; some pretty incredible stuff can grow in the most inhospitable environment, including your organization. Keep pushing on that door and forcing it open so the light can shine in. Even if you don't get it all the way open, you have started it, and those who follow will have to push less, and the struggle will become easier, really. Winning isn't everything, that's true . . . but doing your best is. Have faith and hope that one day your vision will be a reality–never lose that hope.

SECTION 5

Have a life outside your department

In three words I can sum up everything I've learned about life. It goes on.

~Robert Frost
poet

> *If only I'd known that one day my differentness would be an asset, then my life would have been much easier.*
>
> ~**Bette Midler**
>
> *singer, actress, and comedian*

Your life is not your job! I know how easy it is to get wrapped up in a career and let it morph into being a big part of you. I saw this a lot in the fire service with firefighters who made the jobs their lives and their lives the jobs. They'd forget they had a life outside of it and they needed to grow the part of themselves not tied to the fire service. The adrenalin rush experienced regularly as a firefighter is an easy drug, which we can become addicted. Everyday we did something different— no two calls were alike. It was a high to say I walked into burning buildings and saved lives for a living. It was a rush like no other I have ever felt. I knew how easy it was to make firefighting my identity.

When I retired, one of the most difficult things was to find a way to let go of my need for adrenaline.

It was my addiction. I had been on its high for most of my career, supplemented with the drama of the lawsuit. I had become dependent on it for my self-esteem and self-worth. Suddenly, I was home: no one cared who I was and I wasn't saving lives anymore. No more burning buildings, just burnt dinners and housework. Who was I? Did I matter to anyone any more? What was it all worth?

Again, I was thankful I had spent a lot of time in "finding myself" before I retired. It has been hard to shift out of that work mode and it's been even harder to re-enter the job market. I had to deal with a lot of fear that the same treatment I had in the fire service would follow me. I want to be a part of something but I'm afraid of being rejected again and having to fight for inclusion. It is that fear I continue to fight now. I have to remind myself there is a world out there that might just want me–that I'm not damaged goods. On one hand, I laugh at myself. *For God's sake, Gina, you were a battalion chief! How can you think you wouldn't be worth anything?* It's a byproduct of my PTSD—I still feel fear under the surface, lingering, leaving me wondering if it will creep up again to strangle me. I know intuitively that isn't true, but my brain still plays with the thoughts every now and then.

I finally had to take the pressure off myself and give myself permission to take time off from having a job. That's a tall order for a Type A person! I had to give myself permission to be lazy, unmotivated, and directionless, and it scared me in the beginning. The thoughts that went through my head on a daily basis kept me feeling like I should be in a mental hospital for the rest of my life. But it has also been good. I have learned to let go and just *be*, to be all right with my body as it is, with my feelings unfocused, free to roam as I choose. I am getting back in touch with who I really am without all my roles and responsibilities. I am healing, and that is a good thing.

I am so thankful to be able to step out of the race for a moment or two and for recognizing I need to heal and be whole before I move on. I used to tell people jokingly that when the case settled, I would be done with the department. I never knew how true that statement would become. Within months of settling, I knew I needed to move on. I was having a conversation with one of the Deputy Chiefs whom I liked and had worked with on diversity issues. While sitting in his office, the subject of diversity came up. He asked me if I thought there were still some issues within our department. I got righteous and said, "Yes, there are still some issues!" He looked at me with great concern and asked me what I thought those concerns/issues were. He wanted insight and help in correcting them. I told him after stumbling around a bit that I would have to get back with him with a list and left shortly after. As I got into my battalion chief's vehicle, I thought to myself, *What a coward I was! I couldn't even give him a list of things yet I was acting all wronged!* I realized in that moment I had become a dinosaur. I was a product of the past and I had already given all I had. Times *had* changed and it was time to step down and let the others present their ideas and claims. It was my time to say, "When."

As I reflect back on all I have written, I want to tell you, the readers, you are so worth it! Remember, you are worth being treated with dignity and respect. It saddens me that we still have issues with race and gender, yet I marvel at the fact this nation elected its first African-American president and a woman ran a fantastic race for that very same top office. We have come a long way, baby! Hilary Clinton's concession speech was one of the best I have heard touching on diversity. I loved when she said there might still be a glass ceiling for a woman being president, but now there were 6 million cracks in it. I feel the same way about my work with the fire department. It became clear to me that the glass ceiling was in my way for advancement beyond battalion chief. I had once aspired to be the fire chief and when I gave up on that goal, I gave up in a lot of other ways too; the challenge and excitement was less, more subdued. My decision to give up going for fire chief coincided with the settlement of the case, but I think it was already there before we settled. I believe I would have made a good Fire Chief, but not in my department, as things felt too raw for all involved. I have since decided to explore my other creative talents and see what this next phase and chapter of my life brings. There are lots of cracks in the ceiling in my old department concerning diversity, thanks to the hard work of lots of good women (and good men), and one day they will have a woman fire chief, or at least a woman chief above battalion chief on the suppression side of the house. I know they will be ready for it because the pioneers who have gone before have already started to pave the road and put cracks in the ceiling. That door will never be shut again.

Regardless of your situation, even if it is extremely challenging and stressful, remember you are worth it. Take care of yourself, your family, and your friends. In the end, that's who we really have. Work friends are just that, friends from work. No one cares what you used to do. They care what you are doing right now. Have fun in this journey called life. It improves with time! It's funny, I spent so much time being the "best lil' firefighter I could be" and yet at the end, when I became more authentic and cared less about what they thought of me in the department, I enjoyed some of my best times and connections there. Be yourself, your true self, and have fun. As Joe Dirt would say, "Life's a garden, dig it!"

As I close, I leave with you the words of Marianne Williamson. These words are not only beautiful but express my wish for each and every one of you . . .

Our Deepest Fear

Our deepest fear is not that we are inadequate. Our deepest fear is that we are powerful beyond measure. It is our light, not our darkness that most frightens us. We ask ourselves, who am I to be brilliant, gorgeous, talented, fabulous? Actually, who are you not to be? You are a child of God. Your playing small does not serve the world. There is nothing enlightened about shrinking so that other people won't feel insecure around you. We are all meant to shine, as children do. We were born to make manifest the glory of God that is within us. It's not just in some of us; it's in everyone. And as we let our own light shine, we unconsciously give other people permission to do the same. As we are liberated from our own fear, our presence automatically liberates others.

So go forth and shine!!!

Sincerely and respectfully,

Gina Geldbach-Hall

Lessons that come easy are not lessons at all. They are gracious acts of luck. Yet lessons learned the hard way are lessons never forgotten.

~Don Williams Jr.
novelist & poet

You have to wonder about the city planners that put Pepcon, a rocket fuel plant, right in the heart of a residential neighborhood. What were they thinking? Sure, it might have been fine if nothing happened, but Murphy's Law always seems to prevail eventually. And it did on May 4, 1988, when all hell broke loose. Tragically, yet miraculously, only two people died the day Pepcon exploded; the lesson learned—we no longer have a rocket fuel plant in the heart of our residential population. My department's "Pepcon" was February 2, 1987, when they hired four strong-willed, capable women who really wanted to make a difference as firefighters for their department and their community.

Who would have thought this would set off a chain of events that would lead to major changes in how they ran the fire department? The lessons learned by the department during that time are still being integrated and the next generation of men and women firefighters will have to continue the legacy of integration and equality. The good news for women firefighters to come is the foundation has been laid in the blood, sweat, and turnouts of their sisters before them. The light in the doorway is shining brightly, just keep pushing, sisters!

I want to personally send a big *thank you* for all the inspiration and encouragement I received from the women who went before me and candidly shared their struggles for equality. You are my shero's and I am the recipient and legacy of your journey. *It won't be forgotten . . .*

I also need to thank the men who supported and encouraged me (and other women) along the path. It was your heartfelt love and support that kept the door open and helped push us through. Your vision and compassion truly made a remarkable difference and for that I am eternally grateful. It takes two to tango and the dance was amazing!

Many people will walk in and out of your life, but only true friends will leave footprints in your heart.

~*Eleanor Roosevelt*
First Lady

It is so true . . . by the time you are through with any journey, there are many people to thank along the way. No one travels alone, and I am no exception.

Some that have helped make this book a reality and I owe a great deal of gratitude are the three editors I had work on this book, Amy Mitchell, Carol Holaday, and Judi Moreo. Thank you, Amy, for teaching me how to write and really pushing me to explore my creative talents; Carol, for making the "magic" come alive and making this a published success; and, Judi, for being my grammar police and arresting all my bad habits! All of you have made this journey enjoyable *and* presentable and I am so glad you all were part of this ride.

My thanks and gratitude goes to my main two lawyers, Kathleen England and Don Tingey. Over way made me feel like I wasn't alone. Thank you . . .

To my friends who were my greatest supporters! Neva and Carl Liebe, for being my son's second parents; Wendi Thompson and Peggy Glock for being life-long wonderful friends; Lily Brand and Lisa Kane for being there and listening to my growth, one onion peel at a time! Thanks to Carol Reynolds (CarolReynolds.com), who was a powerful motivation in moving me in another direction and helping me realize I can take risks and be okay. You truly changed my life. Thank you, Destiny Retreats (DestinyRetreats.com), for teaching me how to connect with my inner self and how to breathe. Tammy Lord, for opening my eyes and helping me start a journey, which totally changed the *who* I am . . . thank you. There are many other supporters along the way and I will miss most but thank you . . . Rhonda Huskey-Dehner (for the heavenly angels advice), Renee Dillingham (for keeping the pit bull on a leash and trying to teach me politics!), Joe Cathey (for keeping me laughing and not beating me up!), and Heather Steele (SteeleCoach.com) for sharing yourself and your tremendous gift of love and coaching to the world; you've helped me see the light of day on more than one occasion.

To my other supportive friends who are dear to my heart . . . Mary, Russell, Renee T, Louanne, and Jerry (for being my spiritual family), Michael Johnson (you've made me believe in myself again and opened me up to a new and wonderful life), Dr. Janet Bixler (for keeping my head and heart intact and functioning at its best), and lastly, Lari McSwain. Lari, you were a better friend than I ever was–the perfect one to have. I miss picking up the phone and talking, knowing you would understand what this book's journey is all about. I truly miss your kindred spirit . . .

To my family, a simple and heartfelt–thank you. You provided the foundation that gave me the strength and resilience to make choices based on my heart. You have stood by me when I was not so lovable and cheered me on to go out one more time and put myself on the line. I want to thank my two beautiful and loving sons, Joe and Dylan Hall; you are my greatest achievements in this lifetime. I also want to thank my ex-husband, Brent Hall. You stood by me when most men would have run and for that, I am very appreciative. It was both of us together that turned out some pretty fabulous children and along the way carved out some pretty good memories as well . . .

Lastly . . . to this day I am still at awe and admire the men and women who make up our fire and emergency services. I am proud to say I was a part of that family. Without them, this story would not have been possible, the good and bad. At the end of this journey, my thoughts linger on the honor and valor I saw from them daily in dealing with situations no person or people should have to endure, and they did it with grace and dignity. No matter what, they were prepared to go the distance, *and*, they did make a difference. My heart goes out to all of you and I wish you a safe and speedy trip home to your families and friends at the end of each shift or run. Be safe out there, you truly are shero's and hero's . . .

Gina Geldbach-Hall is an inspirational keynote speaker, award winning author, consultant, and seminar facilitator with 25-years of emergency services experience from EMT and firefighter to battalion chief. She holds degrees in Fire Science Technologies, Fire Service Management and Bachelor of Science in Business Administration with an emphasis in Marketing and Advertising. Gina is also a graduate of the Department of Homeland Security, National Fire Academy, Executive Fire Officer Program. She currently resides in Las Vegas, Nevada, where she values time with family, her two wonderful sons, and friends. She continues to inspire leadership and service helping others to ignite the flame of empowerment within their lives and work.

Gina is available for speaking engagements, book signings, and seminars. If you would like to attend one of her programs, check her schedule online for availability and locations near you. To request a seminar or personal appearance in your area, visit her website at:

Sign up at Gina's webpage for her blog and newsletter. Look for her next book(s) coming out soon. *Firegal . . . Lessons from the Fire Line*, second book in the Firegal three part series, and, *Fireproof!* Using the fire department system for success and organization in project management and small businesses.

To receive her, *52 Tips from the Fire Line*, weekly inspirational messages on how to improve your own leadership and empowerment skills visit:

52TipsFromTheFireLine.com